Bruce Muster

To a really, really
sweet guy!

an
Enclave
of Elegance

an Enclave of Elegance

A SURVEY OF

THE ARCHITECTURE, DEVELOPMENT AND PERSONALITIES
OF THE GENERAL ELECTRIC REALTY PLOT HISTORIC DISTRICT

*profusely illustrated with OLD PHOTOGRAPHS
and ARCHITECTURAL DRAWINGS never before published
as well as many NEW PHOTOGRAPHS
by FRANK TEDESCHI and EDWARD BRUHN.*

by

Bruce Maston, M.D.

Published by G.E.R.P.A. Publications
in cooperation with
The Schenectady Museum
Nott Terrace Heights
Schenectady, NY 12308

Library of Congress
Catalog Card Number: 83-81556

John Moore Graphic Design, Delmar, NY
Argus Press, Albany, NY

ISBN 0-9613352-0-3

This book is dedicated to my daughter Sarah and her generation. They will benefit from the awareness that this book will foster.

3

Contents

Prologue

Schenectady was founded as an agricultural and fur trading center by the Dutch in 1662. In spite of an Indian massacre which burned this early stockade in 1690, the "Old Dorp" (the Dutch word for town) slowly grew into an important center of commerce during the eighteenth century because unnavigable falls north of Albany at Cohoes made a portage necessary in the movement of goods and settlers between the Hudson and Mohawk Rivers. At the western gate of this land bridge, Schenectady reaped the commercial benefits from the brisk traffic through the major water connection between the seaboard and the western interior. With the completion of the Erie Canal in 1825, the water route became continuous, and Schenectady lost its advantage as a transfer point. Later in the 1800's, Schenectady again became an important terminus as the railroad replaced the Erie Canal. Locomotive manufacturing was its major industry in the middle years of the century, but even with this base, the Old Dorp was a small town of 13,500 in the year 1880 as compared to Albany's 91,000.

The major turning point in Schenectady's history was the establishment in 1886 of Thomas Edison's Electric Machine Works, which later became the corporate giant, the General Electric Company. While Albany grew steadily to 113,000 in 1920, Schenectady's population exploded to 20,000 in 1890, to 32,000 in 1900, to 73,000 in 1910, and to 89,000 in 1920. This has given Schenectady an urban landscape quite different from that of its near neighbor as large tracts were developed rapidly to house the influx of new employees.

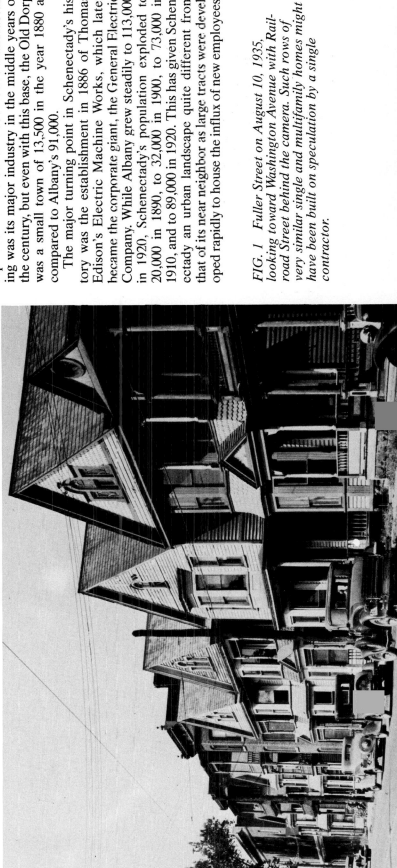

FIG. 1 Fuller Street on August 10, 1935, looking toward Washington Avenue with Railroad Street behind the camera. Such rows of very similar single and multifamily homes might have been built on speculation by a single contractor.

5

Even the most casual observer will notice a sharp contrast between the quaint streets of the original Stockade area and the rest of the city that is dominated by block upon block of frame houses of very similar construction (fig. 1). For further reading on Schenectady's history, the author refers the reader to any of Larry Hart's excellent books such as *Tales of Old Schenectady, Vol 1.*

Shortly after the area known as the "GE Plot" was rezoned as the General Electric Realty Plot Historic District in 1978, the idea grew that a book should be published to acquaint visitors as well as long-time Schenectadians with the significance of this special neighborhood. While contractors were putting up frame dwellings for the flood of workers coming to the burgeoning Electric Works, a pressing need arose to provide suitable homes for the upper echelon of the company. This book will describe the planned community that resulted. The original thought was a modest pamphlet to discuss the most "famous" individuals who lived here and to punctuate it with a few pictures of some of the homes. But as old maps and photographs began to surface during the early phase of the project, I began to believe that every house was worthy of inclusion and that all the past residents had made significant contributions, either locally, nationally, or internationally. The scope widened further when I contacted James Kettlewell, an architectural historian at Skidmore College in Saratoga, New York. After he generously shared his knowledge of the architecture of this period with me, I realized that the book could also serve as a handbook to a fascinating architectural era. Most of the "old houses" still standing in this country date from the late nineteenth and early twentieth centuries, yet very few books dealing with the architecture of the period mention residential architecture. Emphasis shifts to the monumental Beaux Arts style (figs. 2, 3) or the skyscraper. This leaves most

FIG. 2   The Brooklyn Museum of Science and Art, by McKim, Mead, and White (1895-1915), built in the classical Beaux Arts style of the late nineteenth century.

people with no understanding of the old residential styles which are most prevalent today. Through examination of the houses of the GE Realty Plot, it is possible to comprehend the evolution of residential architecture beyond the Victorian period.

This book is mainly about buildings because the Realty Plot consists of buildings. But there is more to the significance of the area than its architecture. The people who lived here made important contributions. Acknowledging the contributions of these notables, unfortunately, presented problems. First, even through the story is only 80 years old. I was unable to find information on many of the owners. Families move away, and obituary notices tend to distill a person's life to a list of fraternal organizations and job titles. This information does not tell a story. Second, many of our famous residents worked in technical, scientific areas which mean little to the general public. For instance, Dr. Irving Langmuir won a Nobel Prize, but his work remains arcane to all but fel-

FIG. 3   The Schenectady Trust Company, Brandywine Avenue and State Street, built 1927 by L. Rodman Nichols. Bankers, even conservative, clung to Classical motifs, derived from the Beaux Arts style, well into this century. This building, much smaller than the Brooklyn Museum, would still not be suitable as a home. Through neither building can we interpret most residential building.

low chemists. I have tried to interpret these accomplishments to construct an entertaining story about the area.

Admittedly, this book could have been written to emphasize different points. Inevitably, it is written about things of interest to me.

Bruce Maston, M.D.
The August Weber House
February 9, 1983

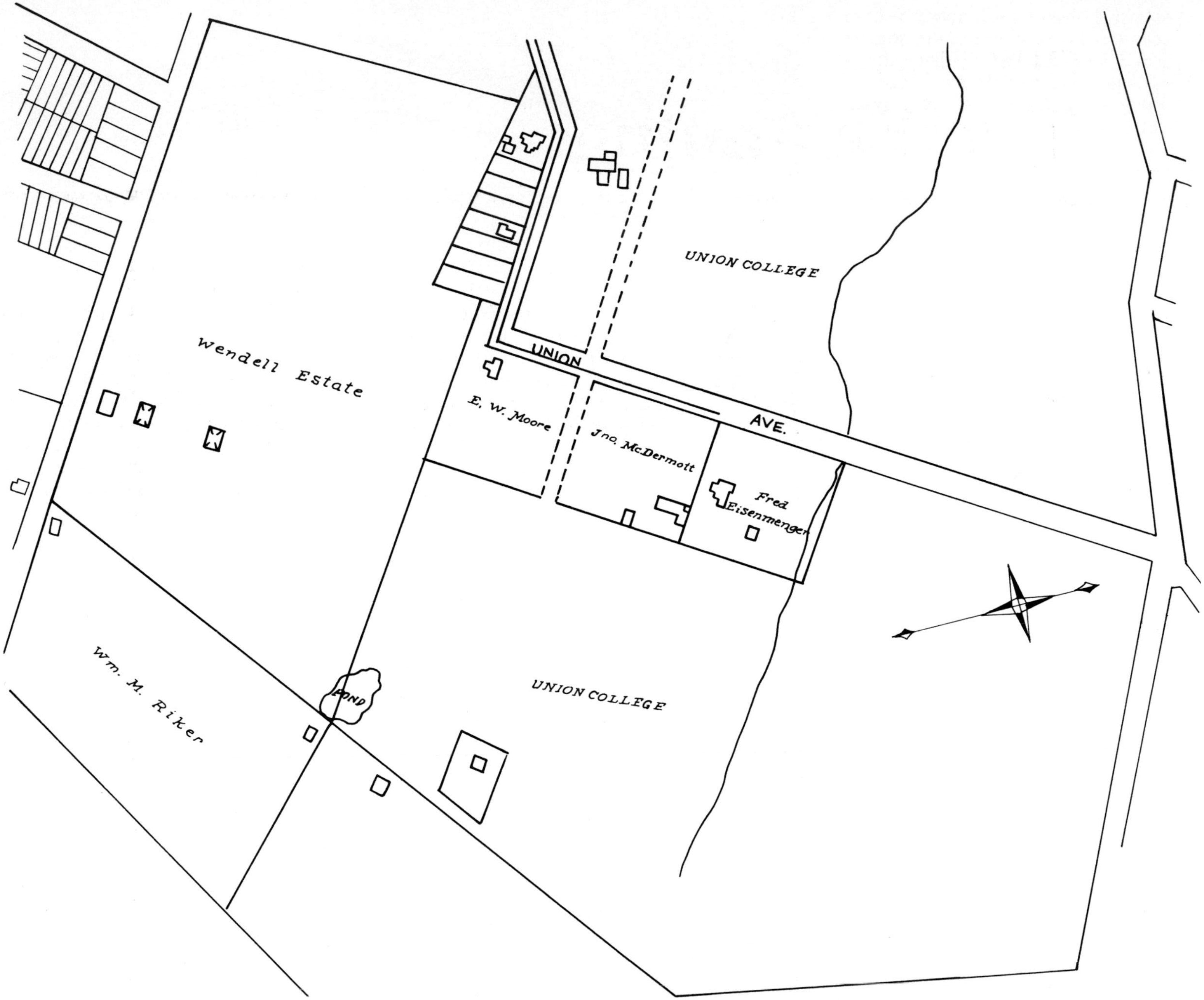

Wm. M. Riker

POND

Wendell Estate

UNION COLLEGE

E. W. Moore

Jno. McDermott

Fred Eisenmenger

UNION

AVE.

UNION COLLEGE

CHAPTER I

The Beginning

*The White Rabbit put on his spectacles.
"Where shall I begin, please your Majesty?"
he asked. "Begin at the beginning," the
King said, very gravely, "and go until you
come to the end: then stop."*

Alice in Wonderland
Lewis Carroll

 On March 1, 1899, the Schenectady *Evening Star* printed an announcement by John DeRemer, representing the Board of Trustees of Union College, that the College would sell a 30-acre tract to the west of the campus, known as the "College Pasture," as well as a 75-acre parcel to the east called the "College Woods" (fig. 4). Then as now, money was a problem for the College: there was a $30,000 debt to be liquidated. Something must have been afoot as the paper editorialized that this represented an opportunity for an "enterprising syndicate" to purchase the land and establish some first class "villa-style" homes.

Fifty-five prominent citizens had other ideas about how this opportunity might be exploited. On March 16, they met at City Hall to propose that the land be used as a park; a committee consisting of W.T. Hanson, A.P. Strong, and E.C. Angle was formed to negotiate with the College. Union College and the committee proposed that the city lease the land. By today's standards, tentative lease terms of the lease agreement would have been generous—$5000 per year in perpetuity for the 30-acre College Pasture and $3000 per year for the larger College Woods. A petition drive to purchase the land for a park achieved an astounding 2200 signatures, the largest such drive in Schenectady's history to that time. Meanwhile, on March 26, it was announced that another group had first option on the 75-acre tract to the east of the College, and on March 30 the General Electric Company announced the purchase of the College Woods for construction of homes for its employees at the substantial price of $57,000, or $750 per

acre. This was hailed as a philanthropic gesture as it wiped away Union's debt. Noted the *Evening Star*, "Some ultrasensitive sons of Union who have never put their hands in their pockets to help the alma mater may possibly regret this curtailing of the grand old property, but her most loyal sons, with the knowledge of the beauty, extent, and sufficiency of what will still remain, will hail with joy this action of the trustees." (The attempt to lease the remaining 30 acres came to naught when the City Council rejected the proposal because of the cost and the flat, marshy nature of the land. It would be two decades before Mayor Lunn established a park system in Schenectady.)

Several of the principal directors of the General Electric Company, including names we will meet later in this book, formed a subsidiary corporation called the "Schenectady Realty Company" to carry out the actual purchase and development of the land. The land was deeded to the Schenectady Realty Company on May 6, 1899.

The area was completely undeveloped at the time of the sale (figs. 5, 6).[1] Surveying began in the spring of 1899, but the work of grading the roads, laying water and sewer lines, and constructing the bridges was not completed until August, 1903. The portion west of Wendell Avenue was offered for "inspection and purchase" on September 8, 1899.

The term "landscape architect" was first used by Frederick Law Olmsted, Sr., in connection with the designing of Manhattan's Central Park. By 1900 the profession of city planner was being recognized. Advocates of the "City Beautiful" movement sought to improve the appearance of even

then decaying, overcrowded, industrial districts which were seen as incompatible with America's emerging role in world affairs. Broad boulevards, parks, and impressive buildings, they argued, would provide not only visual appeal and recreational areas for citizens but also uplift them in such a way as to increase respect for the ennobling arts. They even took it as an article of faith that well-designed cities would lower crime rates. (The recurrence of this same impulse was responsible for the urban renewal movement of recent years.) Examples of the City Beautiful movement can be seen in present-day Washington, D.C. and Chicago. Classical formalism and symmetry domi-

nated the thinking of planners due to an all-pervasive nationalism which saw mighty America as the new Rome. Schenectady's Parkwood and Glenwood Boulevards were conceived along these lines with two wide streets radiating from a central plaza.

The design of the Realty Plot was executed by the firm of Parse and DeForrest (fig. 7). Instead of choosing the axial plan which would be applied in the design of the new boulevards off Union Street, they drew their inspiration from New York's Central Park and followed the older picturesque method of landscape design (fig. 8). The surveyor later wrote that the Plot was visualized as con-

FIG. 5 *Photograph of the College Woods dated Oct. 12, 1899. The house in the middle background, the E. W. Moore house in Fig. 4, orients us. The camera is near the corner of Douglas Road and Lenox Road, facing southeast.*

sisting of two smaller plots divided by Wendell Avenue. Using Wendell as a baseline, roads were laid out in gentle curves. To heighten the park-like atmosphere, sod gutters were selected in preference to curbs. "The sod gutter," wrote the surveyor, "was a rather untried experiment on public roadways outside of parkways where it had been used to a small extent. The effect is very fine in could be plowed without disturbing the gravel sidewalks. An area behind the Brown School was flooded each winter as a skating pond for the exclusive use of Plot residents, who were issued lapel tags. A special hydrant was installed for this and is still visible. Around 1912, the city took control of street maintenance under the influence of Socialist Mayor George Lunn, and concrete sidewalks were installed to reduce maintenance costs. Mr. Grosso's son recalls that this "took away some of the unique character of the neighborhood"—apparently there was, indeed, some coherent effect to the street plan as originally devised.

An important aspect of the original concept was the inclusion of restrictive convenants in the deeds to control how the property could be developed. (Restrictive covenants are effectively the same as zoning ordinances, with the difference that instead of the building inspector or zoning board telling a property owner what he can do on his land, the deed of the property contains a list of restrictions to which the owner agrees when he buys the property.) The Schenectady Realty Company's covenants stipulated that no building lot could be less than 70 feet by 140 feet, no fences higher than 3 feet 6 inches; no building closer than 25 feet to the road, nothing but a single-family dwelling; and, most important, no house costing less than a stated minimum. In the early years the dollar figure was set at $4000 or $5000. With inflation, this figure was gradually raised in later years, but many of the houses built in the Plot greatly exceeded the minimum cost. These were indeed posh homes— by comparison, in the spring of 1905, the average house in Schenectady was built for around $2700.

The fence covenant has an interesting background. In England, fences were commonly set on the perimeters of country estates: meant as barriers, they tended to be very high and crowned with glass shards or spikes. In this country, a three-foot fence was purely ornamental; it could not keep anyone out, but it could make an important contribution to the design by framing it (fig. 11). Foreign visitors marveled at the lack of high fences here, a symbol of the freedom of our classless

FIG. 6 *Another view dated Oct. 12, 1899. The exact location is uncertain. This and the preceding photographs were taken from General Electric archives and were labeled "Schenectady Realty Company."*

that the roadway is bordered by grass and no curb is there to mar the effect" (fig. 9).

The surveyor also mentioned that the absence of curbs presented a maintenance problem, and two men with a team were required to rake and mow the gutters in the summer and to remove snow in the winter. The two men were Paul Grosso and William Clute. Mr. Grosso was performing grounds maintenance work at the General Electric plant when he came to the attention of H.W. Darling, Vice-President of the Realty Company and overseer. Grosso began as gardener and coachman in Mr. Darling's house on Wendell Avenue, but soon a fund was established by all the owners

and administered by Darling to perform all general maintenance (fig. 10). The tasks included seeding and caring for lawns, setting trees and shrubs, hauling trash, and cleaning walks. William Clute was the drayman who, with a team of workhorses, cleared snow from the streets and pulled away trash and ashes. Two-by-twelve inch cleated planks were laid each fall so that the snow

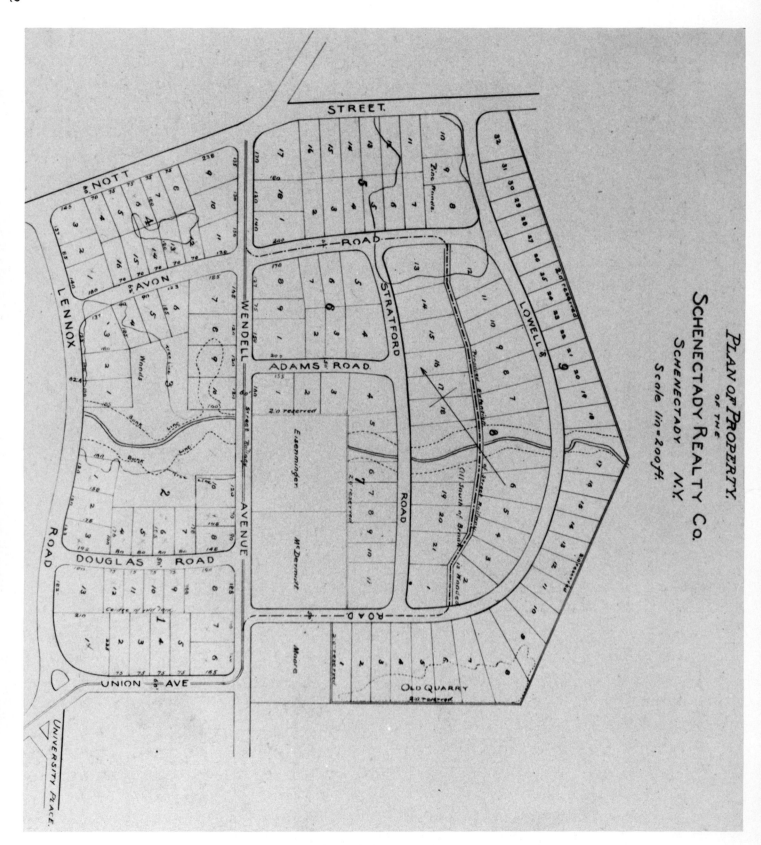

PLAN OF PROPERTY.
OF THE
SCHENECTADY REALTY Co.
SCHENECTADY N.Y.
Scale 1 in = 200 ft.

FIG. 7 *An early plan for the Realty Plot dated*
December, 1899. Note the absence of Rugby
Road.

FIG. 8 *Central Park in an 1865 lithograph by*
John Bachman.

13

LENOX ROAD, SCHENECTADY, N.Y.

FIG. 9 Postcard view of Lenox Road looking south. The ravine bridge is visible in the middle distance. The picture was taken before cement sidewalks were installed.

FIG. 10 Paul Grosso standing by the porch of the Darling house.

society. Tall fences were thus excluded, not only because they would defeat the carefully planned vistas of the curbless streets but also because they were undemocratic!

One problem the Realty Company had to face was the bridging of the thirty-foot-deep ravine through which flowed what was known as "College Creek" or the "Grooteskill" (kill being the Dutch word for stream). This was accomplished at four places with arched bridges of Duanesburg bluestone (fig. 12). The bridges were intended to be barely visible from the roadway; as with the sod gutters, the hand of man was to be kept invisible.

How were the street names chosen (fig. 13)? An explanation survives, written by Henry W. Darling. He and George E. Emmons were a two-man committee charged to select the names. Nott Street pre-dated the development and bore the name of Eliphalet Nott, the illustrious president of Union College for sixty-two years. In June, 1899, a road was opened from Union Street to connect with Union Avenue. The City Council renamed the entire street Wendell Avenue, after a Miss Wendell, whose house once stood on Union Street and who owned "a considerable tract of property through which the street was made" (See figure 4). Wrote Darling, "What was then known as . . . the 'Quarry Road' in pursuance of the plans of the Schenectady Realty Company was opened up as a 70-foot [wide] roadway eastward, with the exception of the part fronting on the property owned on either side by McDermott and Moore, where it was only 44 feet wide, and these property owners refused to give an inch more to widen the road." This was then called "Union Avenue East," but was subsequently changed by the City Council in 1904 to "Rugby Road" because of an open area at the corner of McClellan Street and Rugby Road where the game was played.

There were yet six roads to be named by Mr. Darling and Mr. Emmons. They considered and discarded the names of the original settlers and Indians because they were already commemorated in some way. Darling felt that the names should have a "tangible connection" and "submitted for

FIG. 11 The stone wall around the Darling house on the corner of Wendell Avenue and Nott Street defines the property as separate from its surroundings. This wall has an elaborate decorative top of varicolored jagged stones bordered by smaller smooth stones.

FIG. 12 The Lenox Road bridge has a twelve foot, full-centered arch just the width of the road, viz: 62.5 feet.

FIG. 13 The 1901 map outlines by double lines the holdings of Eisenmenger, McDermott, and Moore. Names on the map indicate the lots purchased to that time. The earliest completed section was the "western plot" below Wendell Avenue. Some changes had occurred in the earlier plan (fig. 7), most notably the construction of what would become Rugby Road.

FIG. 14 Lower Avon Road. This photograph was taken from Charles P. Steinmetz's balcony between 1903 and 1908.

consideration the great rivers of Europe, the rivers of England, the English lakes, and the names of Sir Walter Scott." "It was decided to use Sir Walter Scott's names, but Mr. Emmons insisted that the names of some men famous in the history of New England might also be perpetuated, and so two roads—Adams Road and Lowell Road—represented these worthies, and the others—Lennox Road, Douglas Road, Avon Road, and Stratford Road—had their origin in this way." So much for committees! The "characters of Sir Walter Scott" seems pulled from the air to us today; but the committeemen were deeply rooted in a Victorian heritage. Nineteen original owners were named either "Albert" or "Edward," presumably after the Prince Consort or the Crown Prince; the Victorians, as we shall shortly see, were very taken with an idealized medieval past, and when we look at the homes that Mr. Darling and Mr. Emmons built, we will hear the distant echo of Ivanhoe's gallant steed.[2]

Lennox Road is today spelled with only one "n." The original spelling appeared on maps in 1901, 1905, and 1912, and a petition from residents to "City Council requesting street numbers used "Lennox" in 1904. Another rambling petition dated 1903, however, employed "Lennox" and "Lenox" interchangeably. The 1903 city directory used the double "n," but thereafter switched to "Lenox." There is no record of an official name change, so apparently the postman and the homeowners lacked Mr. Darling's same fidelity to literary sources and the shorter spelling has prevailed.

Figure 13 shows the final arrangement of streets as well as three large parcels on Wendell Avenue la-

beled "Eisenmenger," "McDermott," and "Moore." As Union College had already sold this property in the 1880's, it was not part of the seventy-five acre tract conveyed to the Schenectady Realty Company. This explains the refusal of McDermott and Moore to allow the widening of Rugby Road mentioned above in Darling's account. The Realty Company must have been acutely aware of this salient of land not governed by the restrictive covenants. In fact, in 1912, it purchased the northern portion of Eisenmenger's land and sold it to Edward Waters, who built there in 1914. Because of the lack of covenants, a few of the houses on Rugby Road are closer together on smaller lots; but, by and large, this did not become a problem to the Realty Company. The whole area is now within the boundaries of the Historic District, and it includes some of our most important buildings. The narrower section of the road can still be seen.

So, we have seen how a unique combination of circumstances, the financial exigencies of Union College on the one hand and the need for an exclusive residential section on the other, led to the formation of the Realty Plot. In 1903, the surveyor claimed, "We have here a suburban residential plot second-to-none between New York and Chicago, either in layout, restrictions, or the class of houses upon it" (fig. 14). The task of the remainder of this book is to examine the architecture of these houses and note the achievements of the people who dwelled in them. Before doing so, however, we must briefly survey America's building traditions to be able to understand how these buildings fit into the sequence of architectural evolution which today constitutes our visual heritage.

[2] In spite of Darling's explanation, the names have a suspiciously Shakespearean sound. True, Douglas is a character used by Scott, but Lennox must be a minor character, indeed, as none of the standard reference works on Scott mention him. On the other hand, Lennox does appear in "Macbeth" and warns him of MacDuff's escape.

CHAPTER II

Architectural Background

When the first settlers arrived on the Atlantic seaboard, they brought with them the traditional building styles of their Northern European homeland. Buildings from this period are called "medieval" by historians even though they were built well after the end of the Middle Ages. The House of the Seven Gables, constructed in 1668 by a sea captain in Salem, Massachusetts, is such a building (fig. 15). Because of the importance of the term "medieval" to the rest of this book, let us explore this at some length.

True medieval buildings dating from before 1400 share a number of traits. To begin with, they are asymmetrical, being shaped to fit the lot size or needs of the owner. An aspect of this asymmetry is that the windows are of irregular size and arrangement. They are placed in such a way as to let in maximum light. It was to be a later preoccupation to construct symmetrical houses with central entrances and predetermined numbers of regularly spaced windows. Another hallmark of medieval buildings is the prominence of a steep-pitched roof, designed to carry water and snow off the house. Last, they have large distinctive chimneys, prominent in the overall appearance. This prominence is only natural as the hearth was central for cooking and warmth. The medieval builder, then, was concerned only with warmth and security. He paid little heed to "design;" he was the member of a guild and built according to methods handed down through centuries of tradition. Foremost in his disregard of "style" was a central philosophy that ignored this world in favor of the spiritual one to follow.

Beginning around the year 1400 in centers of learning in Italy, in concert with a rise of trade and prosperity, a new outlook emerged which questioned doctrine and turned with a renewed interest to the secular culture of ancient Rome and Greece. This shift to secularism, "the Renaissance," was reflected in the emergence of a new architecture that drew its inspiration from Classical design. But this changed outlook took time to travel from Italy to the more backward countries of Northern Europe, and still longer to travel down the economic ladder from wealthy merchants to the class of people who emigrated to our shores. In fact, it took more than 300 years and thus it is that the House of the Seven Gables is "medieval." The medieval character of early American houses is masked today for several reasons. First, the earliest buildings were rude huts, and they were later torn down as the colonies began to prosper. Second, because the older techniques used in Europe were inadequate for our climate, many houses did not survive. Third, as time went by, the medieval style was viewed as horribly out of date, and houses were remodeled to conform with new fashions.

As noted, the Renaissance style took time to reach other areas. It did not fully reach England until after the Great Fire of 1666, when Sir Christopher Wren began rebuilding London in the Renaissance manner. There had been awareness of what was happening in Italy, but Wren's visual demonstrations enthralled the aristocracy who wanted to achieve the same effects in their own homes. Since the resulting building boom took place during the reigns of the three Georges, we

FIG. 15 *The House of the Seven Gables. Note its prominent asymmetry, steep roofs, and large chimney.*

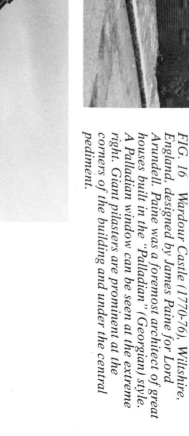

FIG. 16 *Wardour Castle (1770-76), Wiltshire, England, designed by James Paine for Lord Arundell. Paine was a foremost architect of great houses built in the "Palladian" (Georgian) style. A Palladian window can be seen at the extreme right. Giant pilasters are prominent at the corners of the building and under the central pediment.*

call this style not "Renaissance" but "Georgian."

What were the typical features of an English Georgian building? There were many, of course, but we shall focus on only a few. There was the "hipped roof" which has four uniformly pitched slopes. There was the "Palladian" window with its high-arched central window flanked by lower rectangular windows. Finally, in the later Georgian, there was a tendency to interrupt the roof above the central entrance with a triangular pediment, and giant or colossal pilasters (columns) decorated the building (fig. 16). This English Georgian style reached America only in a watered-down version (fig. 17).

The Revolutionary War interrupted all building in America. When construction resumed after 1783, a new style had developed which we call the "Federal" style.[3] It is also termed the "Adam" style, not after the American family that spawned two presidents but after the Scottish architect, Robert Adam. The Federal style is easily confused with the Georgian because they share many common elements, but there are differences. One difference in the Federal style was the fan-design, low-arched window over the doorway; another was the prolific use of decorative, slender swags or garlands. Rural houses employed conventional gabled roofs instead of hipped roofs, and oval windows were common on the gable ends. The whole façade was much plainer and lacked bold pilasters; paired porches appeared which employed slender, paired colonnettes (fig. 18). The Federal style was more decorative, especially on the inside, and drew its inspiration not from public Roman buildings but from the private villas then being excavated at Pompeii.

Beginning around 1830 and extending to around 1850, Americans became dissatisfied with a frilly style that eulogized a decadent Rome. They once again sought pure Classicism and settled upon Greek models, specifically Greek temples. This "Greek Revival" period coincided with a national temperament that likened the rugged, democratic settlers of the New World to the citizens of the city-states of ancient Greece. The hallmark of a

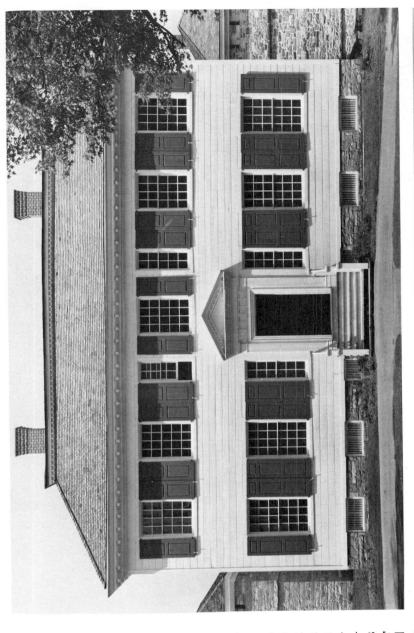

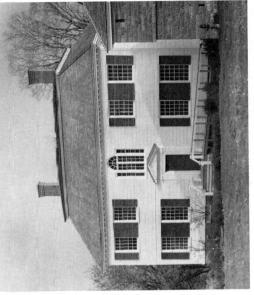

FIG. 17 *Johnson Hall, built 1763, for Sir William Johnson near Johnstown, New York. The house pales in comparison to Wardour Castle, but is remarkable considering it was situated in a wilderness surrounded by frequently hostile Indians. The wooden siding was incised to resemble costly stone.*

FIG. 17a *The rear of Johnson Hall shows us a classic Georgian-style Palladian window.*

[3]*World War I had a similar effect on the Realty Plot. Only three homes were built between 1915 and 1919, and the houses built after 1920 are of a different style.*

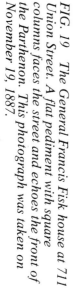

FIG. 18 The "House of History," Kinderhook, New York (c. 1819-20) by (?) Barnabus Waterman. A low-pitched roof has been concealed behind a balustrade in this rural house. Architects in our century use models such as these in reproducing Colonial architecture.

Greek Revival building is its lack of arches—the Greeks did not utilize them (fig. 19). The entrance has a rectangular window across the top with two vertical windows flanking the door. Also typical are simple Doric columns, frequently square, which have no ornament at the top. Upstate New York was settled during this period, and our countryside is riddled with these buildings with their almost tract-like similarity. We were also left with such Greek city names as Utica, Ithaca, and Troy.

It was this sameness that led to the emergence of the Victorian style around 1840. The Victorians found the stark white Greek temple design to be incongruous with its surroundings, reasoning that a country house should blend into its environment. In their Romantic view, a battered, abandoned, medieval castle covered with vines and blending into the environment symbolized the truths that could be gleaned if man would live in harmony with nature. Nineteenth-century Romanticism was a reaction to eighteenth-century Rationalism. Victorian architects rejected the Rationalism embodied in the Greek Revival style. There are numerous periods and movements in the Victorian style which lasted from 1840 to 1900. The only one that needs concern us is the very last one, termed the "Queen Anne" style, which commenced around 1880. Before discussing this style and the houses in the Realty Plot fashioned in the Queen Anne style, we should note those elements which, in general, typify it. Actually, the list is no more than a reiteration of the characteristics which mark the medieval style with which we began. That steep-pitched roofs, asymmetry, and massive chim-

FIG. 19 The General Francis Fisk house at 711 Union Street. A flat pediment with square columns faces the street and echoes the front of the Parthenon. This photograph was taken on November 19, 1887.

FIG. 20 *The Watt Sherman house by H.H. Richardson (1874-75).*

FIG. 21 City Hall, Albany, New York (1880-82) by H.H. Richardson. This building is called "Romanesque" because of the heavy round arches. Richardson made a study of Romanesque churches as a student in France.

neys reappear in this period is no coincidence, since Victorians looked to the Middle Ages for inspiration. We are drawing very near now to the planners of the Realty Plot and their street names taken from Sir Walter Scott.

Different architectural historians have used various terms to describe the Queen Anne period. The first term, "shingle style," describes buildings—usually featuring large, wrap-around porches, bay windows, and asymmetrically placed turrets and dormers—which are covered with shingles (fig. 20). Henry Hobson Richardson, the most important

architect of the period, popularized their use. He was seeking an American architectural form, and the shingled house had rich associations with early New England homes. He also desired a uniform, neutral surface to pull together the disparate design elements of his asymmetrical buildings. In defining a "shingle style," one singles out but one building material used in the Queen Anne period.

"Richardsonian Romanesque" is another term frequently used to describe this period. Richardson's style has little in common with early medieval churches except for his similar emphasis of massiveness with rock-faced masonry and with round arches. In addition, he introduced a number of stylistic elements soon copied by a host of imitators (fig. 21). Because Richardson died young (in 1886), and because he frequently delegated work in his busy office, he actually had total responsibility for only a small number of works. Thus, most "Richardsonian" buildings, even ones designed in his own studio, are no more than an assemblage of the stylistic features of his few authentic creations. Further, the style was so enormously popular that all Queen Anne buildings contain some elements borrowed from Richardson. Shingles, the large round arch, the short column with its characteristic carved capital, rock-faced masonry—these are details we will meet again and again (figs. 22, 23).

"Queen Anne" is used here to designate the late Victorian period. This term includes the terms "shingle style" and "Richardsonian Romanesque." It originated in England in the 1870's and is associated with the architect Richard Norman Shaw. Once again looking into the past for inspiration, Shaw chose the last period of medieval architecture in England immediately before the Georgian style, i.e., the reign of Queen Anne. Really, though, it would be easier to think it the "Queen Elizabeth" style, as Queen Anne buildings usually feature the half-timbering we associate with the Tudor period. When the style arrived here, it was modified by Richardson by the inclusion of rock-faced masonry, New England shingles, and other elements mentioned earlier to create an American Queen Anne style.

FIG. 23   Staircase of the Charles G. Ellis mansion on lower Union Street. Typical Richardsonian motifs, such as a round arch are here moved indoors. A fireplace located in the entrance hall is another innovation by Richardson; it recalls the massive hearth of the medieval period. Several houses in the Realty Plot have such fireplaces near the entrance. This stairway was demolished to be replaced by a steel staircase to meet fires codes.

FIG. 22   The Edward Ellis house (left), 215 Union Street, and the Charles G. Ellis house (now Amity Hall), 217 Union Street, both completed in 1885, are excellent local examples of Richardson's Queen Anne style.

FIG. 24   *The Jones-Eisenmenger house (c. 1883),*
1226 Wendell Avenue, as it appeared in 1926.

CHAPTER III

The Queen Anne Style

In 1884, Walter A. Jones encountered "severe financial difficulties." The Jones Car Company, manufacturers of railroad and trolley cars, was sold at a public auction in which even the "eloquent auctioneering," of a Mr. Palmer could bring no more than $30,000. Adding to Mr. Jones's misery, he was compelled to surrender his partially-completed residence to satisfy three notes, totaling $933, for the lumber used in the building. Jones had purchased five acres from Union College in 1882-83 and had begun construction of "Brookside" in a pine grove beside "the brook that bounds through Union's grounds." Newspaper accounts relate that a handsome villa had been planned to embrace the "Queen Anne" and "Old Colonial" styles, along with "many new and attractive features." The building was purchased and completed in 1887 by Frederich Eisenmenger (Eisenmenger was to be the Mayor of Schenectady from 1904 to 1906).

This home exemplifies the salient features of the Queen Anne style (fig. 24). There is a horizontal, spreading quality which separates it from earlier Victorian styles which are more vertical in feeling. An all-embracing roof, its eaves curving upward and running together to a climactic peak, pulls the composition together. The ground floor is of masonry construction—in this case brick with half-timbering—while the upper story employs the characteristic shingles. A massive, decorative medieval chimney breaks through the roof line. Round arches are used not only in the doorway, but also on the attic gable. This latter arch contains multiple panes of "bull's-eye" glass, a colonial motif

(fig. 25). Glass was immensely expensive in colonial times; so, to trim costs, the unusable crown of the glass-making process was used around doorways. It was too uneven to be seen through, but it did admit light into the hallway. Here, this irregular glass is used as a decoration in a unique location. Victorian architects borrowed freely from the past but were always careful to use old ideas in novel ways so that they could not be accused of plagiarism. In another instance on this house, a baroque scroll pediment which would properly appear atop a Chippendale highboy has been blown up and placed over the second-floor triple window. Topping the building is a fantastic custom-made tile dragon. Where the architect got this idea is known only to him, but the dragon is a familiar theme of the historical Queen Anne period as Europe was inundated by Chinese trade goods. Probably, the architect decided to place a proper Queen Anne dragon at the summit of the proper Queen Anne house!

Next door at 1204 Wendell Avenue is a house built, circa 1896, by John McDermott (fig. 26). The McDermott house is much simpler than the previous one, yet it remains typically Queen Anne. The original design included a wrap-around porch which has been removed in favor of the smaller version. The result, noticeable even to the untrained eye, makes the building look "too tall." Examples such as this show the folly in attempts to "modernize" or "improve" old houses. From what we do see, the building is a *tour de force* of bricklaying. The main building consists of common bond in which the bricks are laid end-to-end

in the "normal" fashion, while the turret employs Flemish bond in which every other brick is laid with the small end exposed (fig. 27). The doorway is highlighted with a lighter-colored brick. Above the windows the brick forms a segmental half-arch which is not only decorative but also functional in supporting the building. Dominating the design is a tower with a "candlesnuffer" top, a standard tower design of the Queen Anne period. The building can be viewed as a conservatively designed "vernacular" house, probably not architect-designed but built by a skilled contractor who has displayed his craft in the home.

This fits nicely with what we know of John McDermott. He had worked for seven years as a mason and later established a contracting business which operated from 1867 until his death in 1916. McDermott was the most successful contractor of his day. His buildings include St. John the Evangelist Church and the County Courthouse. His first major buildings were the McQueen Locomotive Works, allowed to lie idle when one of the partners died. It was these vacant buildings which attracted the attention of Thomas Edison, and they became the nucleus of the General Electric Company (fig. 28).

The first home in the GE Realty Plot built as part of the planned development was the spacious home of Edwin Wilbur Rice, erected in 1900. In the early days, the electrical industry seems to have been a family affair, for E.W. is the first of three Rices we shall meet. E.W. Rice was the second President of the General Electric Company, from 1913 to 1922; he also held over one hundred patents (fig. 29). In 1893, he recruited Charles

FIG. 25 *Unusual "bull's-eye" glass decoration of the Jones-Eisenmenger house. When window glass was hand-blown, the unusable portion around the blow-pipe was used around doorways. The Jones-Eisenmenger dragon consists of cast pieces of ceramic tile. The tile industry was at its zenith during this period. A wide selection was available, and custom-made pieces such as this one could be commissioned for a modest additional cost.*

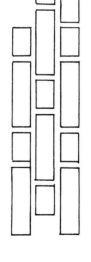

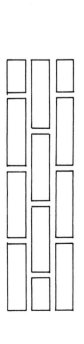

COMMON BOND

FLEMISH BOND

FIG. 27 Bricklaying patterns—Flemish bond and Common bond.

Steinmetz for the company's engineering staff, and in 1900 he recommended the formation of the Research Laboratory. Of particular interest to this narrative is that he was the President of the Schenectady Realty Company. His house occupies five choice lots on the Realty Plot's most prominent corner; it commands the view of anyone coming into the area from downtown (fig. 30).

The house is classic Queen Anne style, and it could also properly be called "shingle style." A Victorian architect would have called this style "picturesque"—by which he would have meant that the parts of the building were arranged the way a painter arranged a landscape composition. The "picturesque" freely placed things where they "felt good." No two areas of the design were the same, just as no two parts of a landscape were identical. As in the House of the Seven Gables, the basic effect here is generated by the asymmetry of the gables. The E.W. Rice house also demonstrates several motifs widely used by Richardson. Shingles were used to unify a Queen Anne design as well as to recall colonial New England. The windows are of the standard Queen Anne type—broad with multipanes above and single panes below; there is also a tendency to group the windows

FIG. 26 The John McDermott house (c. 1896). Because no building permits were needed before May, 1905, houses built prior to that can be difficult to date. In this case, review of tax records shows a rise in the assessment to include a house between 1895 and 1897.

FIG. 28 The McQueen Works were purchased by Edison for his Electric Machine Works.

FIG. 31 Rock-faced masonry layed in an intricate jigsaw pattern is a characteristic feature of Queen Anne architecture.

in banks. Somewhere on any Queen Anne building we can usually find rock-faced masonry with an intricate pattern of large and small stones. Here it forms the masonry of the foundation (fig. 31).

On another impressive corner stands "Hillcroft," the home of Henry W. Darling (figs. 32-34). This Queen Anne structure is so heavily injected with eclectic Victorian motifs that it defies exact classification. By now we can recognize the Queen Anne use of brick in the first story (with the half-timber work, this time, appearing in the second floor). Semicircular bays enriched with stained glass pass through all stories in the high Victorian fashion. In total, the design seems more Continental than English because the decorative half-timbering, coupled with "bargeboards" (fig. 35) terminating in carved heads, is reminiscent of a German town house where such gable ends face the street. The Victorian architect very frequently

started with one historical period in mind and then noticed the similarity of his design to some other historical period. He delighted in grafting details from the second period onto his original design to create a hybrid.

The completion date of 1901 is very late for the construction of such an eclectic Victorian home, but this may relate to Darling's background in the conservative world of finance. H.W. Darling, born in Scotland, migrated with his family to Canada in 1863 at the age of sixteen. The son of a farmer, he entered the import-export trade and thereby acquired experience in foreign exchange. His acumen in business and finance led to his rapid rise in financial circles in Toronto. From 1883 to 1886 he was President of the Toronto Board of Trade and, from 1886 until 1890, he was President of the Canadian Bank of Commerce. After 1882, his Canadian home was a castellated residence called "Hillcrest," which may explain the name with which he christened the Schenectady house. The 1880's were halcyon years in Toronto for the Darlings, but in 1890 Darling lost his presidency in a power struggle at the bank. He was a fiscal conservative—one of his supporters came all the way from Winnepeg to cast a vote for "Mr. Darling and sound investments"—but other directors viewed his leadership as sluggish in that expansive period in Canada. Then, too, Darling had instituted a management training program—ultimately to his disadvantage because it provided a successor at hand. Much later, at General Electric, he was asked why he did not train an able assistant in case he should wish a leave of absence. Replied Darling, "I once whittled a fine stick, and it was used to give me a beating."

After his ouster from the bank, Darling's career waned only briefly. His expertise in finance had gained the attention of the Edison Electric Company, and he was retained to help consolidate the various small Canadian utilities in which Edison held an interest. After the merger of the Thomson-Houston and Edison Electric companies in 1892 into the General Electric Company, Darling was first made Assistant Treasurer. In 1894 he was

FIG. 29   Edwin W. Rice (1862-1935), second
President of the General Electric Company.

FIG. 30   The Edwin W. Rice house (1900), 102
Lenox Road: The predominance of shingles on
the exterior has led Queen Anne houses of this
type to be termed "shingle style," but shingles
appear somewhere on most Queen Anne houses,
and even this house incorporates many other
Queen Anne traits in addition to shingles.

FIG. 32 "Hillcroft." Written in Darling's hand on this photograph: "A young fellow 'speeled' the telephone pole on the Ave and grabbed this, then sold me the negative for fifty cents."

named Treasurer, a post he held for thirty years (fig. 36).

H.W. Darling was vigorous, brilliant, devoted to his family, egocentric, and opinionated. His grand-daughter, Helen Henshaw recalls, "When I was twelve years old, I had scarlet fever and was quar-antined with a nurse in my bedroom. Grandpa D. sent me a postcard in the mail every day, and one day father put a ladder up to my window. The dear old man climbed up to look at me through the window." He was an original promoter of the Mohawk Golf Club, but he lost interest because the sport could be played on Sunday. He was Vice-President of the Schenectady Realty Company. To him fell the responsibility to see that the builders complied with the various restrictions; he is said to have used a hammer to test the quality of bricks being used. He was an excellent horseman from his youth, and he maintained the stable at Hillcroft into the 1920's. Each day he was delivered and retrieved from his office in a landau. Decorously dressed, he would step into his carriage amidst a crowd of pedestrians and motor vehicles and, with a crack of the whip from his mustachioed coach-man, would be driven home at a dignified pace.

Darling's enterprise had an impact on the com-pany from its inception. During the panic of 1893, the new industry was near bankruptcy. It could not pay its debts because those to whom it had extended credit were themselves strapped. One firm in Chicago owed $50,000; Darling traveled there to visit its president as this money was desperately needed, but he found that the com-pany had little promise of remaining solvent and

FIG. 33 Early view of the Darling house from Wendell Avenue. Note, in the left background, the absence of Ellis Hospital, which was built later; note, also, the carriage house which was later demolished.

FIG. 36   Henry W. Darling, Treasurer of the General Electric Company for thirty years. Portrait taken around 1905.

that its only asset was the rugged integrity of its aging owner. Darling struck a bargain with him that General Electric would not pursue its claim if he would name it beneficiary of a $50,000 life insurance policy. When the executive died a few months later, General Electric was the only credi- tor that did not lose money. Following this panic, and throughout his long career, H.W. Darling worked to ensure a sound financial base for the company. In 1912, it made final restitution to all stockholders who had suffered in 1893 by declar- ing a 30% stock dividend.

The English Queen Anne style drew its inspira- tion from pre-Georgian England and usually in- cluded some Georgian motifs, symbolizing the truly transitional nature of a period lying between the medieval style and the Renaissance-inspired

FIG. 34   H.W. Darling house, north side.

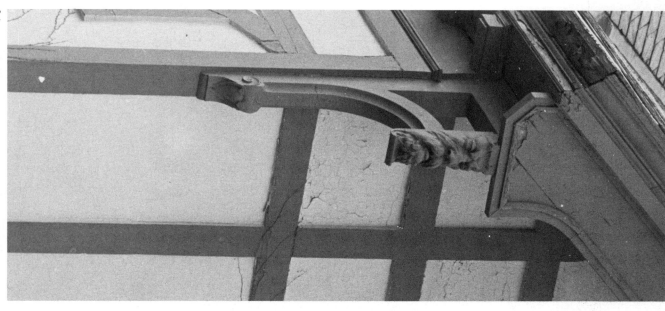

FIG. 38   The Harry W. Hillman house (1901), early photograph.

FIG. 35   A bargeboard with carved figure on Hillcroft. A bargeboard is a decorative board covering the face of a projecting gable rafter.

FIG. 37   An oval window with fan design. This window design is taken from the Federal period, not the Georgian, but architects of the American Queen Anne style included motifs taken from any early period in the nation's history.

FIG. 39 *The Theodore Button house (c. 1904) has a heavy, horizontal quality which was intended to convey a feeling of the house's attachment to its surroundings. H.H. Richardson made extensive use of cut stone to impart this weighty feeling, but the effect could also be achieved, as here, with shingles.*

Georgian style. In the American version, elements drawn from Colonial architecture could be substituted for exclusively Georgian designs. This explains why the Jones-Eisenmenger house was described as being built in the "Old Colonial" and "Queen Anne" style. The Hillman house (1901), 6 Douglas Road, has a vertical oval window which is actually a Federal oval window turned on end (fig. 37). Over the porch is a triangular pediment displaying a Georgian decorative motif. Round Richardsonian arches in the great porch, wide windows with multipanes above and single panes below, and an overall massiveness or heaviness put this house in the mainstream of the American Queen Anne Style (fig. 38). The style, under Richardson's guidance, sought a massiveness which is lacking in the English Queen Anne movement. The Jones-Eisenmenger house, built earlier, shows less of Richardson's influence and does not hug the ground as insistently as the Hillman house.

The Theodore Button house (c. 1904), 69 Union Avenue, is similar to the Hillman house (figs. 39, 40). Again the porch has an arcade of round arches, and here surmounting a porch banister composed of field stone. This stonework is identical to the type used in the wall surrounding the Rice house next door, suggesting that the architect purposefully used field stone masonry to carry through the design. Instead of a candlesnuffer top, the tower has a balustrade to match the main roof. Asymmetrical elements in the composition are united by neutral shingle siding.

Colonial motifs here are slightly more evident than before—perhaps the later date is responsible. We can see a Georgian hipped roof and "widow's walk,"[4] the little circular windows in the tower are common throughout Colonial Williamsburg; and "dentil molding"—so called because it resembles a row of teeth—and the broken segmental arch above the dormer window on the third floor are Georgian.

So far we have discussed high-style Queen Anne buildings as executed by architects of the time. But during the same period, many less pretentious homes were being built by contractors without the aid of an architect. Six houses, three on Nott Street and three on Rugby Road, are examples of these "vernacular" homes (figs. 41-46). We can identify them as Queen Anne on several counts. All are assymetrical; all have windows that are multipaned above and single paned below; and, of course, all are shingled.

By reason of their locations, all of these houses were constructed on lots that were less desirable. This may explain why the houses were not elaborate. Nott Street being the boundary of the development, it was not possible for the Schenectady Realty Company to enforce covenants upon landholders across the street. On Rugby Road, some lots were adjacent to an access road into the bluestone quarry from which was obtained gravel for the roads. Possibly the company built them to provide shelter for the workmen, or possibly these houses were built to provide suitable temporary quarters for a succession of new arrivals. High sales prices on some of their deeds (the Clarke house lot was sold by the company for $3750 while an empty lot on Lowell Road as late as 1914 cost

[4] Very few Georgian houses were built by sea captains or even afforded a view of the sea. The notion that these balconies were designed for wives watching for the return of their husbands is fantasy. These balustrades are a purely Georgian decorative treatment.

FIG. 40 *The Theodore Button house, detail.*

FIG. 41 The James P. Felton house (c. 1902), 1010 Nott Street. The prefabricated oriel window under the porch eave on the left is new.

$1400) coupled with some of the sales being subject to existing leases suggest that these houses were commissioned by the Schenectady Realty Company. There are some fascinating similarities to suggest they might all have been built by the same contractor. Most employ paired, square, double colonnettes on the porches. Certainly the Felton and Hanscom houses are identical (Figs. 41, 42). One hallmark of a vernacular house is a casual placement of windows; instead of being located strategically to compliment the façade, they are randomly placed without regard to the final appearance. In the Hanscom/Felton houses, for instance, the second-floor windows do not quite line up with the dormers.

On the other hand, this group suffers only in comparison to smashing compositions such as the Darling and Hillman houses. By themselves, they are above the average vernacular home of the time. The Hanscom/Felton houses display high shingle piers which would become fashionable in the Bungalow style, and the barred screen near the door and barred balustrade on the porch are taken from the related Arts and Crafts movement. The Schoonmaker house (fig. 43) is somewhat different from the preceding two in that a double-gable front has replaced the double dormer, but the feeling is similar. The double-gable is a rare motif; coupled with an anchoring of the second-story windows in a band beneath the eaves, it creates a pleasing design. The Clarke house (fig. 44) has a stately simplicity, with an interesting jettying of the second floor on the left side which is balanced by a dormer on the right. The Carr (fig. 45) and Fraser (fig. 46) houses also appear to come from the same plan, but sophistication is more

FIG. 42 The Perry T. Hanscom house (c. 1901), 1156 Rugby Road. Hanscom was an assistant engineer of the Power and Mining Department of the General Electric Company.

38

FIG. 43   The F.R. Schoonmaker house (c. 1901), 1142 Rugby Road. With the exception of changes to the roof, the design is similar to the Felton/Hanscom houses. Schoonmaker lived here only until 1909 when he built on Stratford Road.

evident. There is an "occult balance" in which asymmetrical elements, such as the bay on the left and the porch on the right, play against each other. The porch roof reflects the line of the gable above. None of these houses has any colonial detailing. We have noted the inclusion of colonial motifs in the Queen Anne style, and we shall see that as the style evolved, colonial detailing took over more and more of the building until an entirely new style emerged. These details, however, were usually expensive extras; in less elaborate homes, pure Queen Anne style tended to predominate.

James O. Carr, an attorney, was the Secretary and Treasurer of the Schenectady Railway Company (whose President, Edward Peck, we will meet later). The company built the city's trolley system, which at one point accounted for 140 miles of track and was one of the most extensive in this country. Expansion of trolley lines was accompanied by extensive court battles and litigation. Old newspapers steadily attest Mr. Carr's battling against irate land owners whose property bordered the tracks or maligned drivers whose horses were hit by the speeding trains. For good or ill, however, the growth of Schenectady occurred along the routes of those now forgotten trolleys, and Mr. Carr's legal talents thus determined the shape of Schenectady.

If the Queen Anne style drew its inspiration from pre-Georgian, medieval models, and if American architects interpreted the style in light of the American experience, then the Jesse Henshaw house (c. 1900), 5 Douglas Road, has the House of the Seven Gables touch (figs. 47-49).

Henshaw was the son-in-law of H.W. Darling, and it was Darling who bought the land and commissioned this house. Jesse Henshaw was a deeply pious man. He was a founder of the Union Presbyterian Church and became a vice-president of the New York State Council of Churches. In 1929, as the Great Depression began to take its toll on this area, he was appointed to handle all charitable donations by General Electric.

Henshaw paid for his education to become an electrical engineer by playing the banjo. From this

FIG. 44 *The Caroline V. Clarke house (1902), 1018 Nott Street, may have been built by a different contractor than the other vernacular Queen Anne houses. The present colors of the house, dark brown shingles and dull green shutters, are authentic to those preferred during this period.*

musical background grew the family's interest in music. His daughter, Helen Henshaw, has been a force in the musical life of the city for many years. At one time, the Schenectady Bell Ringers practiced in this home; a wall of the living room was removed to accommodate a grand piano to accompany them.

Although the house has seven gables and dark shingles to mimic a medieval colonial effect, it adheres to Victorian Queen Anne conventions. There are those wide windows, multipaned above and single paned below—and no true colonial would have had a bay rising through two stories. Finally, the house betrays the design of an architect and not a medieval carpenter in the sustained unity of the composition achieved by careful alignment of the windows into two levels which run around the entire building.

Decorative half-timbering, a frequent feature in the Queen Anne style, is conspicuous in the Edward Raymond house (1903) at 1294 Lenox Road (figs. 50, 51). Some would prefer to call this style "English Tudor" (as we shall see later, the Tudor Revival style evolved directly from the Queen Anne). A precise distinction is not possible as the house is transitional, but the prominent gambrel (double-pitched) roof is straight from the Queen Anne. Note, further, the use of a different material, here shingles, on the first floor. Most of the houses we have so far considered have not varied the material used on the outside from one story to the next, but it was customary to do so.

FIG. 45 *The James O. Carr house (1903), 1056 Nott Street. Carr was attorney for the Schenectady Railway Company.*

FIG. 46 *The Robert H. Fraser house (c. 1901), 1134 Rugby Road. Fraser soon sold to Oscar Junggren who resided here for ten years before moving to Lowell Road.*

FIG. 47 *Early view of the Henshaw house (c. 1900). The windowless gable has no entrance on the inside; thus, it was included only to enhance the design. Note how it is reflected in the porch roof below.*

FIG. 48   *Parlor of the Henshaw house, early photograph.*

41

FIG. 50 The Edward Raymond house (1903).

FIG. 51   *The Edward Raymond house.*

FIG. 49   *Early view of the Henshaw house from the southeast. The two-story bay is visible on the right, and note the twin gables over this bay that are similar to those on the Schoonmaker house.*

FIG. 52   *A.G. Davis (1871-1939), vice-President of the General Electric Company in charge of patents.*

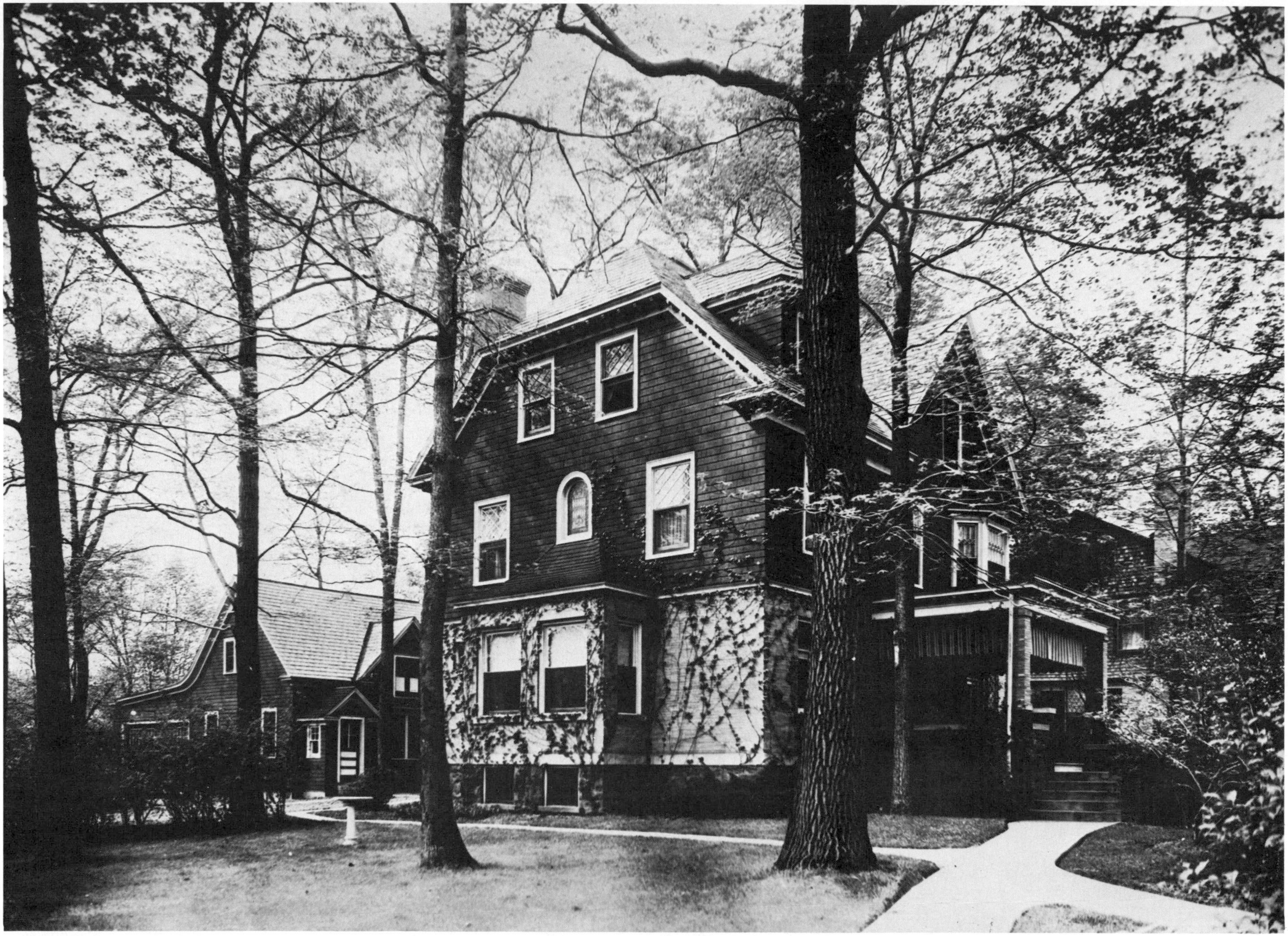

The second owner of this house was Albert G. Davis (fig. 52). Trained as an engineer at the Massachusetts Institute of Technology, he soon moved to Washington, D.C., where he worked in the patent office while attending law school. In 1897, his keen mind attracted officials of General Electric, who offered him the position of manager of the Patent department. He was one of four men responsible for establishing the Research Laboratory of General Electric. New ideas built the electrical industry. Davis's task was to discern which inventions would become indispensable and secure them for the company. During his thirty-five years in Schenectady, he presided over a great flood of pioneer developments.

In light of what we have seen of the Queen Anne style, the August Weber house (1906), 1155 Stratford Road, can be recognized as containing many aspects of the style with its asymmetry, its characteristic window design, its shingled second story surmounting a Roman brick first story, and its use of rock-faced masonry in the foundation (fig. 53). The Richardsonian red masonry has been utilized in building a porch with careful advances and retreats in the design. Another common Queen Anne trait seen here is the "skirting" of the second story in a slight flare over the lower story. The double-leafed front door is the standard Victorian entrance treatment, and the entrance is further enriched with a single inner door containing oval, bevelled glass. This house was built on speculation by Everett Lucas, a foreman at General Electric, who probably lived here in 1907 while finishing the inside or awaiting a buyer. In 1908, the house was purchased by August Weber, Sr., and after his death in 1918, his son, August Weber, Jr., continued in residence until his own death in 1946 (fig. 54).

The Webers—August, Sr., and sons, August, Jr. and John—owned the Weber Electric Company, which at its peak employed about 400 workers. August, Sr., was an inventor and worked with Edison in Menlo Park, but he left General Electric in 1896 to form his own company, which produced porcelain fixtures (fig. 55). (The Depression forced

FIG. 54 Living room, Weber house, as it appeared in the 1930's.

FIG. 53 The August Weber house (1906), photograph taken in the 1930's.

The first story was commonly brick or stone, and the second story shingled or half-timbered, but this arrangement could be altered to the taste of the architect or owner. There is a prominent "jetty" of the second story over the first, frequently described as a "garrison" design because defenders could pour hot oil on attackers through slots in the second floor. Although forts and castles were in fact designed with this feature, here it is taken from medieval town houses where a roomier second story extended over the street.

AUGUST WEBER

FIG. 55 Caricature of August Weber from a 1910 publication entitled Schenectady Just for Fun. *The Weber Electric Company held numerous patents for improvements to the key socket.*

the closing of the company in 1936. In its last three years, the doors were kept open out of consideration for the employees, even though it was operating at a loss.) The house contains numerous outlets, switches, and fuse boxes with the Weber trademark. Weber owned an electric car which he drove daily to the Campbell Avenue plant. His son was a connoisseur of wine and maintained an extensive cellar beneath the carriage house.

The last Queen Anne houses were built in the Realty Plot in 1908 to 1909. At the outset, it was stated that this style lasted from 1880 to 1900. The later dates we have seen here indicate that, at least in Schenectady, the style hung on. Conservative architects or clients perhaps desired houses "like my father built." Changing times were against them, however, and we begin to see changes creeping into the design. For instance, even with exterior modifications, we can see the Queen Anne plan of the Percival Lewin house (1908) at 1327 Wendell Avenue (fig. 56). The design is asymmetrical with projecting polygonal bays and a large tower over the entrance. The second floor skirts over the first, but the ground floor was originally sided with clapboard, not brick. We will see that clapboard was the typical surface used in the following Colonial Revival period.

The Boardman house (1909), 1307 Lowell Road, also contains all the standard Queen Anne features noted earlier, including Tudor style half-timbering of the second floor, flaring-out of the second floor, and the bargeboards described earlier on the Darling house (fig. 35). By 1909, however, there was a pronounced tendency toward symmetry, and, under the Colonial Revival influence, the house begins to assume a geometrical block form (figs. 57, 58). Henry Boardman was the son of a Congregational minister and planned to attend Yale, but he never reached college because an essay entitled "Integrity," written as a senior in high school, earned him an offer to become a bank clerk. Eventually, he became the President of the Schenectady Trust Company (1917-1932).

FIG. 56 The Percival Lewin house (1908). Originally, the second floor was shingle and the first floor was clapboard.

James Fisk Hooker, who did attend Yale, began his career as an attorney, but in 1909, he moved to Schenectady and entered the clothing manufacturing business. His entrance into Schenectady was characteristically splashy as he bought the factory and built his house in his first year here. His factory, the Mohawk Overall Company, employed 200 people. He also served the city as president of the Schenectady Board of Trade and, in 1914, as the City Comptroller. Hooker was related to Jim Fisk, the rail baron, but he seemed to have lacked the family's talent for finance. Large sums were periodically left to him, only to be dissipated in high living and various business schemes. His daughter once proudly showed off a mink coat to her teenage friends, but it was later repossessed.

Later owners of the Hooker house include H. Lawrence Achilles, who directed religious affairs at Union College, and John C. Fisher, a scientist for General Electric who became head of the Bureau of Standards.

This house was built in the Queen Anne style with a shingled second floor skirting out over a stucco first floor (fig. 59). The quatrefoil pattern in the balustrade of the porch is an obvious medieval reference; lead strips hold together the living room windows in the medieval fashion; for further emphasis, Flemish bonding has been used in the brick, as it was in England in the seventeenth century.

The Horstmeyer house (1908), 1198 Stratford Road, imparts a similar feeling (fig. 60). High in the gable end, we see a staunch Richardsonian motif: the group of three recessed windows with shingles curving in to meet them. Elsewhere, freely disposed on this large home, are a tower with a candlesnuffer top and a large wrap-around Victorian porch. A polygonal bay window is perched on the second floor, and opulent construction is visible in the enormous amount of copper used in the porch roof. We have seen that the Queen Anne style could include some colonial motifs; here we see a balustrade on the porch which would have formed the stairway of a Georgian home. The pattern is a standard one taken from a classic architectural text of the eighteenth century.

Yet, there are aspects of the Hooker and Horst-meyer houses which place them in the twentieth century. This pattern of shingles was being used by Frank Lloyd Wright to dramatize the horizontal aspect of buildings (fig. 61). The "fuzzy" brick in the Hooker house was taken from the Bungalow style, and its color is not the red preferred earlier in the period. Both houses are rather too angular for the true Queen Anne; they lack some of the proper "roundness." Nonetheless, these houses could only have been viewed as antiques at the time of their construction.

48

FIG. 57   The Henry Boardman house (1908). This photograph was taken shortly after the house was completed.

FIG. 58   Front elevation of the Boardman house. Boardman chose an architect from New Britain, Connecticut, his home town.

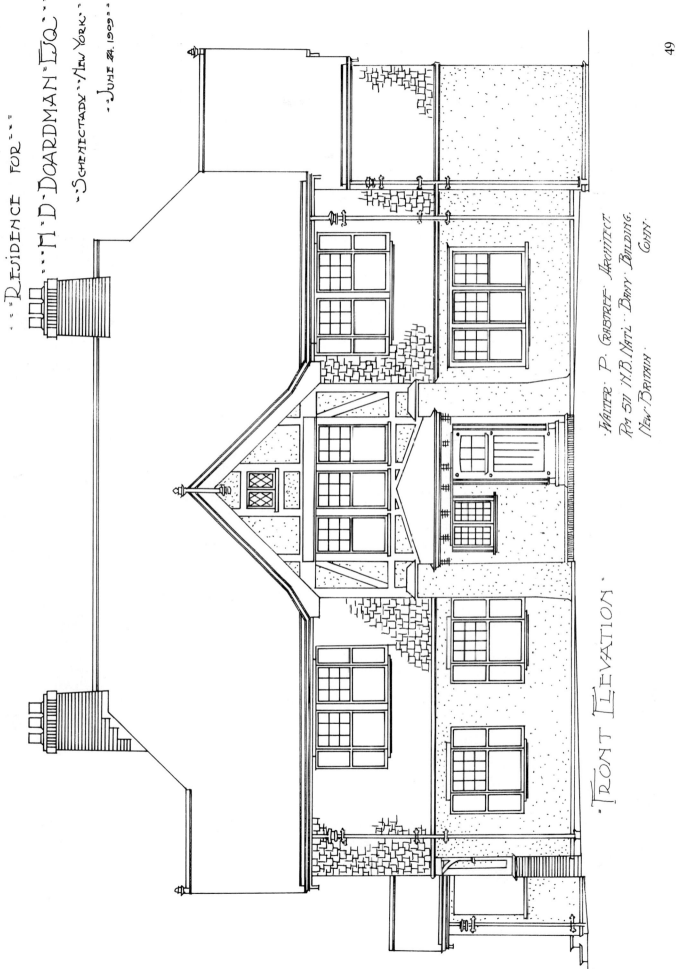

"Residence for"
"M·D·Boardman·Esq·"
"Schenectady·New York"
"June 24.1909"

Walter· P· Crabtree· Architect·
Rm 511 · M.B. Natl· Bank· Building·
New Britain   Conn·

"Front Elevation"

FIG. 59   *The Hooker house (1909), 1181 Avon Road.*

FIG. 60   *The Henry Horstmeyer house (1908).*

FIG. 61 *Shingling on the Hooker house. Dropping alternate rows of shingles creates a banding pattern which gives a more horizontal feeling. This pattern was introduced in the Bungalow style and was widely used in the 1920's.*

FIG. 62 Postcard view looking up Stratford Road from Rugby Road.

53

There can be no fifty-fifty Americanism in this country. There is room here for only 100 percent. Americanism, only for those who are Americans and nothing else.
Theodore Roosevelt
Republican Convention
Saratoga, New York

CHAPTER IV

The Colonial Revival Style

There is never one single cause for any movement in history, whether the movement be artistic or political; and the greater the number of causative factors, the more successful the movement is likely to be. We will see in this chapter that the Queen Anne style was replaced by a style termed the "Colonial Revival" which eulogized the American past. The new style was brought about by a convergence of disparate ideas and developments which all dovetailed so nicely that the practitioners of the style were struck by its "rightness." The Queen Anne recalled a time in England near to the time of American colonial days, and the Georgian motifs we saw on Queen Anne style buildings were recognizable as coming from George Washington's time. In 1876, America celebrated its centennial; this generated a renewed interest in colonial designs. Antique stores today abound with "Centennial" furniture which was accurately reproduced from colonial models. The founding years had been ignored for being rude and uncivilized by the mid-Victorians, but now these objections were overruled by a new patriotism. Interest in preserving such sites as Mt. Vernon dates from the American centennial.

Another converging force leading to the Colonial Revival style came from the commercial and scientific spheres. Expansion into the West, industrialization, and the mercantile energy which was developing the telephone and light bulb, were making this country extremely wealthy. American robber barons like Gould and Fisk made the obligatory Grand Tour of Europe and brought back boat-loads of European art. This plundering was justified in several interesting ways. First, it was seen in Darwinistic terms as natural—the strong taking from the weak. Second, it was viewed as proper that the strong, vigorous, new world of the future should gather and preserve the heritage of the past—in parallel to Rome's borrowing and extending the cultural heritage of the Greeks. It was thought fitting that museums housing these treasures, as well as the government buildings of the New Order, should follow Greek or Roman models, and it was apparent that these models were the same ones used in colonial times. Artists and architects saw parallels between the merchant princes of Wall Street and the Medici, between ingenious American inventors and Leonardo DaVinci, and between themselves and Renaissance artists. They themselves called this period after the centennial the "American Renaissance," and they deemed it fitting to copy Renaissance designs.

The profession of "architect" was also undergoing a change. In the past, architects learned by studying published plan books; but now, with the ease of travel, a growing number were traveling to France to study at the *École des Beaux Arts*. Historically, schools or academies trained by mimicking a fossilized past according to rigid criteria or rules. A steady flow of graduates, therefore, began to return having studied antique forms from the viewpoint of how things "ought to be." Richardson had received some training abroad. His use of eleventh-century Romanesque motifs grew from studying European cathedrals. Another disciple of

FIG. 63 *The Columbian Exposition in Chicago (1893) commemorated the 400th anniversary of the discovery of America. This is a view of MacMonnies's fountain and the Grand Plaza.*

the academy was Stanford White, who initially worked for Richardson and began introducing Renaissance designs into the office's work. Later, White left Richardson so that he could freely express his own ideas. Although a full description of what this system of design entailed would lead beyond the purposes of this survey, it is worth noting that White employed a greater symmetry, with classically proportioned elements drawn from the Renaissance and, ultimately, the ancient world. In 1893, at the Columbian Exposition in Chicago, the firm of McKim, Mead, and White designed many of the main exhibit halls. Just as Christopher Wren's buildings captivated pre-Georgian England, so these buildings were extremely influential in directing the destiny of American architecture (fig. 63). The style is known as Beaux Arts after the school that trained its adherents. So many courthouses and monumental public buildings have been executed in the style that these designs unconsciously provide us with our image of government (fig. 64).

Rather quickly, the Beaux Arts style influenced residential architecture. The Priest house (1900), 1147 Wendell Avenue, will be our first glimpse of the Colonial Revival style (figs. 65, 66). Edward Dwight Priest was a holder of 41 patents and a leading figure in the development of the electric railroad and subway. As his house is far more symmetrical than any considered previously, the uninitiated might date this building to colonial times. But as we study it further, it looks more and more like a Queen Anne building which has put on an outer garment of Colonial motifs. At the base we see the rock-faced Richardsonian masonry. On the south side is a bay window, another Victorian design. The large front porch, taken *in toto* from the Queen Anne, was essential in a time when ladies and gentlemen took refreshments and received callers on a summer day. The Colonial details—the hipped roof, the Palladian window, and the colossal pilasters on the corners—are largely Georgian. But it would be wrong to call this a "Georgian Revival" building. The style eulogized pre-industrial America; no one was too fussy about whether or not a motif dated from before 1776: Georgian, Federal, and Greek Revival were all called "old colonial." Colonial Revival remains a better term, as these buildings will usually contain some references to each of these three "colonial" styles. The Dutch Colonial style was also disinterred, as we shall see when we examine the gambrel-roofed houses. Here we can see exaggerated keystones over the windows that come from the Federal style, as does the balustrade on the front porch. The colossal pilasters we noted were Georgian, but their recessed central panels are from the Greek Revival.

FIG. 64 *Schenectady City Hall (1930-31) by McKim, Mead, and White. This firm was the most famous practitioner of the Beaux Arts style. By 1930, none of the original partners were still associated with the firm, but it continued building in this tradition into the 1950's.*

FIG. 65 *The Edward Dwight Priest house (1900), photograph taken in the 1950's.*

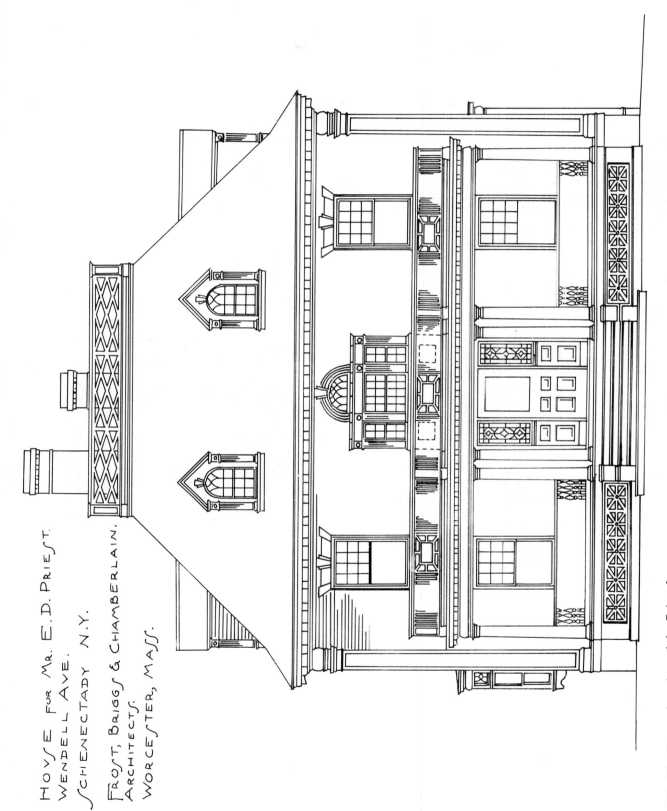

FIG. 66 *Front elevation of the Priest house, designed by Frost, Briggs, and Chamberlain, Worcester, Massachusetts.*

FIG. 67 Horatio Glen (1859-1935).

FIG. 67 Horatio Glen (1859-1935).

FIG. 69 The Glen house (c. 1904), 1144 Wendell Avenue. Early view.

The Glen house (c. 1904) across the street shows the same elements with some variations. In fact, the cluster of buildings at this end of Wendell Avenue are all Colonial Revival, which creates a heightened sense of cohesion. The architectural sequence seems to be part of a grand design suggesting that the Priest house unconsciously triggered a desire in the adjacent owners and their architects to stick with the plan. They recognized—as some are learning today through painful experience—that a neighborhood only "works" when all the buildings are of a similar size and scale. Streetscapes with lots vacant through demolition or occupied by incompatible structures are like diseased hedges.

Horatio Glen, a descendant of the Glen-Sanders clan, was active as an attorney for over forty years after graduating from Albany Law School in 1883 (figs. 67, 68). He served as District Attorney, and, for seven years, as City Clerk. His wife was the daughter of Edgar and Rachel Moore—which explains how he acquired this lion's share of their land adjoining the holdings of the Schenectady Realty Company.

Here the three components of the Colonial Revival are clearly seen (fig. 69). A Georgian Palladian window has been placed in the second story while a Federal fanlight crowns the entrance (fig. 70). The subsidiary porch in the side has the square columns typical of the Greek Revival. During this period, architects were scouring the countryside to find true Colonial models, but there was considerable confusion as to what constituted true Georgian colonial architecture and what had been added later. Thus, the architect here may have felt the side porch was an authentic touch, when in fact the prototype he had in mind was actually a Greek Revival porch tacked on to an earlier building. On the other hand, he may have well understood the inconsistency and have chosen to mix styles in the proper Victorian fashion.

Ida Schermerhorn was the Moores' other daughter. Her house, nestled behind tall oaks, is less conspicuous than the adjacent Glen house. In its quiet way, however, it is a well-designed house

FIG. 70   *A Federal style fanlight window.*

H. G. GLEN

FIG. 68   *Horatio Glen as caricatured in 1910*
in Schenectady Just For Fun.

FIG. 71   *The Ida Schermerhorn house (1901), 1130 Wendell Avenue.*

(figs. 71, 72). We see the broad porch again, this time with Doric columns, and a round-arched window suggesting a Palladian window in the dormer. A Georgian hipped roof is present, but retains a steep Victorian pitch. True Georgian roofs were kept as low-pitched as possible. There are other elements of the Queen Anne. Asymmetry is maintained by the slightly offset doorway, and wide windows, with multipanes above, are retained. Notice how the squareness of those upper panes lends a Colonial inflection; if they were diamonds, they would impart a medieval feeling.

The Colonial Revival, at its finest, had more diversity than the prototypes which inspired it as the Victorian continued to pick and choose elements to suit his fancy. The Blackwell house (1900) at 1050 Avon Road shows more of the versatility of the style (figs. 73, 74). Asymmetry is stronger here. The west wing on the right, with its two-story porch and square columns, is completely in the Greek Revival. The projecting central piece with pediment and pilasters is Georgian, while the porch itself uses slender colonnettes of the Federal. A singular feature for the Realty Plot is the flat board surface used on the central projection (fig. 75). This is called "matched boarding," as opposed to the usual clapboarding in which the siding overlaps. Matched boarding was used on some of the early houses in this country because its flat surface could be scored to resemble costly stone (see figure 17).

Although built a few years after the ones we have been looking at, the Mann house (1906) on the corner of Lowell Road and Rugby Road is similar to these others in its abundant use of colonial detailing (figs. 76, 77).

The Manns must have been an interesting couple. Arthur Mann was an electrical engineer

FIG. 72   *The Schermerhorn house.*

FIG. 73   *The Francis O. Blackwell house (1900).*
This house underwent major renovation in 1927.
As can be seen from figure 14, the house
originally had a more characteristic hipped roof.

FIG. 74 The Francis O. Blackwell house, west wing.

FIG. 75 Matchboard siding. In colonial times this smooth surface could be grooved to imitate the dressed stone used in fashionable English houses.

with General Electric; Eleanor Mann was a physician. (In figure 78, see her in her horse and buggy on her usual round of house calls. Her office and waiting room were in her home.) The 1905 census reveals that every house in the Realty Plot had one or more domestics. What an anomaly Dr. Mann, the working wife, must have presented. Upon the death of the Manns, the house was purchased by their attorney, James C. Cooper. Judge Cooper's career encompassed tours of duty as County Attorney, City Court Judge, Corporation Counsel for Schenectady, and Surrogate Court Judge.

As with the Blackwell house, the Mann house disregards correct historical placement of the components. Instead, the Palladian windows, pilasters, broad porch, and dormers are freely disposed in the Victorian fashion. The present white color is undoubtedly true to the original and comes from the Greek Revival period. White was not the usual color in the Georgian and Federal styles.

In all these several exquisite examples of the Colonial Revival style, it is worth noting, the ornamentation they illustrate was probably never used to any great degree in this country in colonial times. First, the colonies and the infant Republic

FIG. 76   The Mann house (1906), 1162 Lowell Road.

FIG. 78   Dr. Eleanor Mann on rounds circa 1910.

FIG. 77 The Mann house, detail of south side.

had not been wealthy enough to support construction of such lavish homes. Second, the egalitarian nature of our society had barred a garish display of wealth; the wealthiest merchant took pains to live in the plainest house so as not to alarm his neighbors with his opulence. It is difficult for us today, having looked at Colonial Revival buildings for so long, to realize that, when constructed, their likes were unknown here. "House watchers" should keep in mind that any high-style Georgian building probably dates from this period: with this knowledge, an inspection should reveal some of the telltale characteristics we have been discussing.

With the exception of the Schermerhorn house, all the examples so far derive their energy from detailing. The shape of the building goes almost unnoticed as the eye travels from one ornament to the next. In the Schermerhorn house, we can see the basic Colonial Revival configuration—a symmetrical block with a hipped roof and a central dormer. Stripped of ornament, this basic plan is a common one for houses of the period and can be seen on any older street in the city;[5] A survey of the architect-designed houses in the Realty Plot shows the marvelous ways a similar overall plan could be altered to create new effects. Remembering that all of the Colonial styles also followed some basic plan (such as a Greek temple during the Greek Revival period), we should not be surprised to see the Colonial Revival style employing a standardized design; but what is revealing is that, in spite of a stated intent to revive the past, the basic Colonial Revival design bears no real resemblance to any of its professed ancestors.

The Edward Anderson house (1902), 1135 Avon Road, exemplifies how Queen Anne design elements persisted in the Colonial Revival (fig. 79). The new style can be noted in the hipped roof, central dormer, and block shape of the building. Further, clapboard siding has been used instead of shingling. Clapboarding is one characteristic of

[5] As this book was being readied for printing, a new term, the "American Foursquare," gained favor to describe countless contractor-built, hipped-roof, symmetrical block houses that were constructed from around 1900 to 1920. If it is understood that this term describes a simplified version of the Colonial Revival style (a "vernacular" Colonial Revival style), then the term will create no confusion for the reader.

FIG. 79   *The Edward Anderson house (1902).*

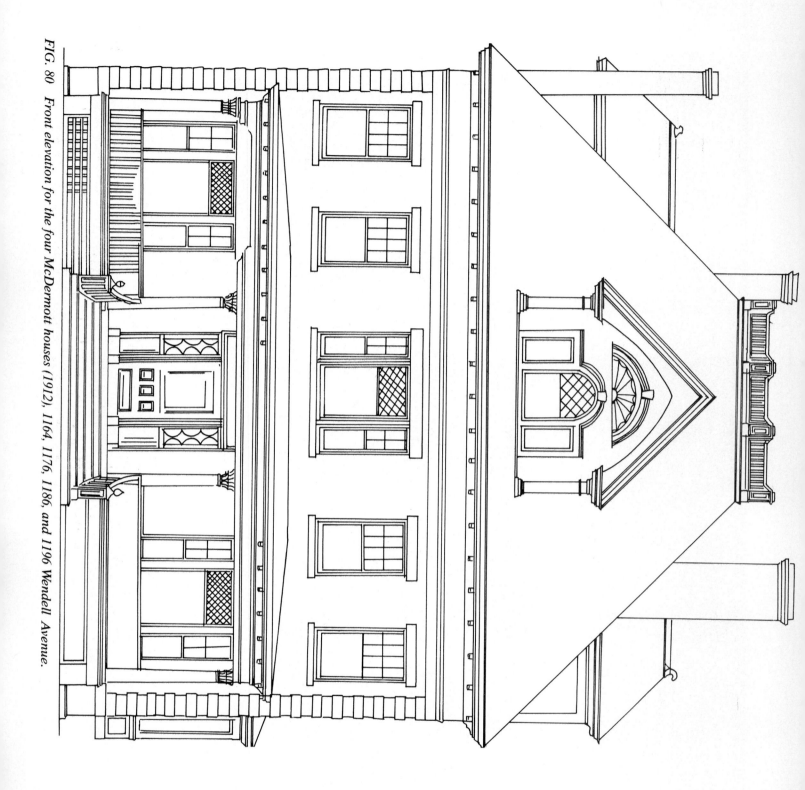

FIG. 80   Front elevation for the four McDermott houses (1912), 1164, 1176, 1186, and 1196 Wendell Avenue.

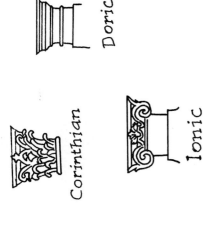

FIG. 82 Column types.

FIG. 83 Porch columns on the McDermott houses terminate in capitals which are a composite of the Corinthian and Ionic orders.

FIG. 81 Leaded, beveled window in front door of 1176 Wendell Avenue. The design is Federal; if split along the long axis and rotated ninety degrees, it would resemble a low-arched, Federal transom window (fig. 70). Not all doors bear McDermott's initials. At 1196 Wendell Avenue, the etched "G" in the center pane stands for "Garrity," the married name of one of John McDermott's daughters.

the Colonial Revival style. Richardson had introduced shingles to evoke a feeling of the colonial past; the Colonial Revival sought to evoke this same feeling but chose to distinguish itself from the Queen Anne with another traditional exterior covering. Still, there are strong elements of Queen Anne styling here. Most conspicuous are the large wrap-around porch, the off-center placement of the front door, and the use of stained glass over the window in the living room. Many houses of the period have such stained glass strategically placed in a hallway or parlor, for at that time the stained glass window was treated as a work of art to be hung on the house the way a picture would be hung on the walls.

In this house, as in all the others of this style, three common traits are manifested: first, a rectangular block design which is distinctly different from the design in any other period and which contrasts with the free asymmetry of the Queen Anne period; second, detailing drawing its inspiration from all three of the colonial periods; and third, the persistence of some elements of the Queen Anne style. Because of the inclusion of some Colonial elements in Queen Anne architecture and some Victorian elements in Colonial Revival architecture, there are numerous instances where precise classification is impossible; but the most consistent litmus test for the Colonial Revival is the hipped roof, central dormer, and symmetrical block.

Like the Queen Anne house of James Fisk Hooker (fig. 59), the four houses John McDermott, the contractor, erected for his children were already old-fashioned when they were completed—in that year (1912), the Colonial Revival style was being abandoned (fig. 80). McDermott had a very clear idea about the permanence of the family. A rear walkway connected all four houses with his own. Symbolically, the family is further bonded because the houses share an identical design and because the color of the brick alternates from house to house. McDermott's experience as a mason explains his preference for this eternal material, and lavish detailing bespeaks a desire to

FRONT ELEVATION.

RESIDENCE FOR
W.M.F. DAWSON
SCHENECTADY,N.Y.

FIG. 84   The Dawson house (c. 1903) in an
unsigned preliminary drawing by the architect.
Because no building permits were required before
1905, the architect's identity is unknown.

FIG. 85   *The John Bellamy Taylor house (1902), 1121 Adams Road.*

Because of its large entrance hall (1/3 the house's width), it was affectionately nicknamed "Mostly Hall" when G.E. bachelors once lived in it.

display material wealth. Each front door has a spectacular beveled leaded-glass window in a spiderweb pattern (fig. 81). The central piece of each window has the etched initials of the original occupant. Other extravagant inclusions are the composite porch columns combining the Corinthian and Ionic orders (figs. 82, 83) and the Palladian window in the dormer. Subsequent economic vicissitudes were unkind to John McDermott's grand scheme. He died without a will in 1916, and the estate was not apportioned until 1927. Soon thereafter, the houses were lost in the Great Depression, and the family was scattered.

The William F. Dawson house (c. 1903), 1131 Adams Road, lacks the extreme embellishment of the McDermott houses, but has a combination of some of the other now familiar motifs (fig. 84). We can recognize colossal pilasters on the corners, a proper Federal style entrance fan light, and the broad Richardsonian windows, multipaned above, single paned below.[6]

Next door, the Taylor house follows the same basic plan, although this has been masked by the later enclosure of the second story sunporch (fig. 85). The house is presently stucco, but this was a later addition over a clapboard surface.

The original occupant was John Bellamy Taylor, who resided here until 1911, when he commissioned another home on Lowell Road. Taylor, an accomplished bassoonist in local orchestras, was also active in the Schenectady Civic Players, often performing in leading roles. In his later years, his hobby of time-lapse photography delighted school children and garden clubs. These were his hobbies. His career as a scientist with General Electric, after he graduated from the Massachusetts Institute of Technology in 1897, was remarkable. He joined the research staff in 1903, and he developed the first equipment to "make sound visible and light audible." Taylor devised a system to transmit sound through a beam of light, and in 1931, he used his "talking ray" to communicate with the dirigible *Los Angeles* as it passed over the Schenectady plant, a feat which gained world-wide recognition (figs. 86, 87). Large-scale commercial uses

of this system had to await the development of the laser beam and fiberoptic telephone cable, but anyone who has ever tripped an "electric eye" in a doorway has experienced Taylor's handiwork. It is said he made the first portable radio by attaching an antenna to the metal frame of an open umbrella so that the receiver set could be carried; he designed many of the early radio receivers. He devised a stroboscopic illumination system to study moving machines, a device familiar today as the timing light used by mechanics to tune automobile engines. In the 1920's, he was instrumental in the invention of the "talking movie," and he devised a successful method for stereoscopic

U.S. NAVY

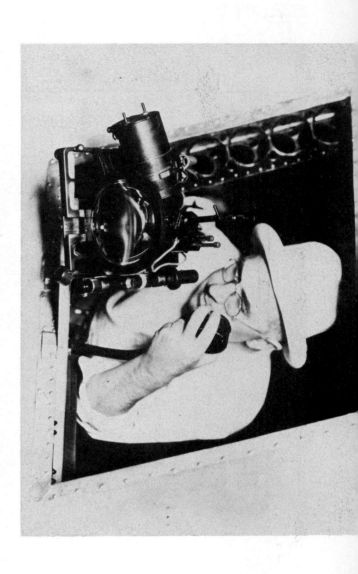

FIG. 86 "John Bellamy Taylor with Transmitter of Talking Beam of Light System in control car of air-ship 'Los Angeles' at Lakehurst, N.J., May 17, 1932."

projection, "3-D," forty years before it re-emerged as a craze in the 1950's.

The Joseph Hoffman house (1903), 1299 Stratford Road, has a symmetrical front elevation, a feature we will note more and more often as the Colonial Revival evolved (figs. 88, 89). A traditional Victorian double-leafed front door readily identifies the Colonial Revival style. The architect was interested in duplicating the symmetry and ornament of the colonial period, but he made no attempt to copy the earlier style. Flanking the doorway are convexly curved sidelight windows; this use of such curved glass is unique for the Realty Plot and was an expensive extra at the time of construction.

The third owner of this house (1920-1935) was George R. Lunn, whose colorful career is familiar to local history buffs. He was born in Iowa and later entered the ministry, graduating from the Union Theological Seminary. "Nature had favored him with a pleasing address and a fluent tongue," and in 1904 he was invited to Schenectady to become the pastor of the First Reformed Church. But by 1909 he was obliged to relinquish his pulpit because his outspoken advocacy of political reform displeased powerful members of the congregation. Later, when a friend warned him that his words in a court case might lead to a contempt citation, he replied, "That is impossible. If anything, I am concealing my contempt for the court." By continuing to speak for the workingman and against corruption in government, he attracted the attention of the Socialist party, and he successfully ran for mayor on their ticket in 1911. Lunn effected many reforms and was re-elected on three subsequent occasions (fig. 90). He also served in the United States Congress and as Lieutenant-Governor of

FIG. 87 U.S.S. Los Angeles in hangar;

FIG. 88 *The Hoffman house (c. 1903), later the home of George Lunn. A large porch once extended to the left and wrapped around the left side.*

71

FIG. 89 *Entrance of the Hoffman house.*

New York State under Alfred E. Smith. His opponents labeled him "a bright cuss, and a good talker, but . . . unbalanced," yet they were no match for either his rhetoric or honesty and concern for the workingman. One Democratic committeeman and office holder went to hear Lunn speak during a campaign and was "well pleased." He went on a subsequent evening, but he left before the clergyman had finished his address. "I didn't dare stay. Had I remained he would have had me sure as I'm a foot high, and I would have looked nice yelling for Lunn and holding the positions I do."

The Robert Duncan Austin house (c. 1904) is located on Lowell Road, adjacent to the ravine. Dr. Austin was a veterinarian, more important to the community than a physician in the days when horses were in common usage. Later, W.V.B. Van Dyck lived here. Van Dyck directed General Electric's operations in South America for fourteen years and was the first and last person to install lights in the Strait of Magellan at the tip of South America. Although this house follows the symmetrical block form of the Colonial Revival, it is interesting to observe how much Queen Anne styling survived in the design (fig. 91). We can see the wide windows, multipaned above, and a masonry first floor surmounted by a shingled second story. Even the skirting out of the shingles was retained. A small, enclosed front porch, executed as a correct Federal imitation, was substituted at a later date; originally, the porch was broader, like the other Colonial Revival porches we have seen (fig. 92).

We now turn to three houses on Rugby Road built on the land owned by Edgar and Rachel Moore. Stephen Visscher moved to Schenectady

FIG. 90 *George R. Lunn (1873-1948). Many of his reforms were long lasting. He appointed a park commission which led to the establishment of Central Park. He inaugurated the nation's first free municipal trash collection system.*

Readers interested in learning more of Lunn's colorful career should read Schenectady's Golden Era, 1880-1930 by Larry Hart.

FIG. 91 *The Robert Duncan Austin house
(c. 1904), 1198 Lowell Road.*

FIG. 92 Entrance of the Austin house.

FIG. 93 The Visschers on their way to church. Mrs. Visscher was an accomplished seamstress and made the dress she is wearing.

FIG. 94 The Stephen Visscher house (1906). Well-proportioned, broad windows enhance the quiet dignity of the design. This photograph probably was taken around 1926.

75

FIG. 95 Molded brick fireplace in the Visscher house.

FIG. 96 The Abraham Brubacher house (1908), 1124 Rugby Road.

from Vischer's Ferry (note the modern spelling) in 1881. He was a founder and President of the Schenectady Savings and Loan, and during his lifetime, he held a record in the state for the longest period of service in a savings and loan association (fig. 93). Of the three houses, Mr. Visscher's, at 1128 Rugby Road, is the most elaborate, a direct result of his keen interest in the final product (fig. 94). The molded brick fireplace in the living room was special ordered by catalogue from Boston (fig. 95). (As the mason was unfamiliar with its jigsaw-like assembly, Visscher had to spend one day with him unravelling its mysteries.) Again we see convexly curved window glass, this time in a bay on the second floor. The combination of a hipped roof with a gable roof is another original touch.

The house next door, 1124 Rugby Road, was built for Abraham Brubacher, who was the Principal of the Schenectady High School from 1905 to 1908 and superintendant of schools from 1908 to 1915 (fig. 96). He left Schenectady in that year to become President of the New York State College for Teachers in Albany, later the State University of New York. During his nearly twenty-five year presidency, he wrote two books, including a four-volume high school English text, *The Spirit of America*.

The house closest to the corner at 1120 Rugby Road was built for Howard Sargent, but for some reason he lived there only one year before building another home on Avon Road. In 1908 George C. Moon purchased the house (figs. 97, 98). Moon's family had arrived in Schenectady prior to the massacre in 1691. He worked for a time as city editor of the *Daily Union* and was publisher of the program for the Van Curler Opera House. As a result of this job, he became a lifelong patron of the theatre; in his later years he spent the first and

FIG. 98   The George C. Moon house (1906). The "X" design of the balustrade is a frequently-used motif of the Colonial Revival style taken from the Beaux Arts style. We have already seen it in the Priest house, and we will encounter it again.

last hour of every day in his extensive library reading Dickens and Shakespeare. In 1910 Moon was elected to the post of County Clerk, a position he held until his death in 1917.

At first glance, the Moon and Brubacher houses look almost identical, but upon closer inspection, small differences become evident. We will see that, as the twentieth century advanced, Victorian pic-

FIG. 97   The Moon children in front of their Rugby Road house. This photograph was taken before the construction of the McDermott houses in 1912. The Jones-Eisenmenger house is visible on the right.

FIG. 99   The Howard Sargent house (1908).
The same architect, Oren Finch, designed his
earlier home (fig. 98).

FIG. 100   Modillions, a Georgian motif, adorn many houses in the Realty Plot.

turesque design steadily lost ground to a desire for ever greater symmetry. We can see the progression here: Moon's 1906 residence has the obligatory second-floor polygonal bay window and an offset entrance; Brubacher's, built two years later, has a more symmetrical façade.

Sargent's second house in the Plot, a grander building at 1136 Avon Road, was designed by the same architect (fig. 99). Comparisons are interesting. The polygonal bay in the second story is retained but has now been placed over the entrance, thus dividing the house into symmetric halves. As with the Brubacher house, a newer style, the Colonial Imitation, is influencing the design. A deeply modillioned (ornamentally bracketed) cornice adds opulence in the Georgian manner (fig. 100). A steep pediment replaces the dormer and suggests the large entrance pediment of the Georgian style. As noted earlier, this pediment, too steep for the true Georgian, reveals its Victorian antecedents.

In the John T. Broderick house (1902), 1079 Avon Road, further original twists can be seen to the basic Colonial Revival design (fig. 101). The polygonal bay on the left, not matched on the right, forms a platform for a small balcony off a second-floor bedroom. The entrance is centrally placed, but recessed, with only a tiny extension for the front porch. Through this arrangement, the actual porch depth is in keeping with the usual depth favored in the period; and there is yet another partially covered balcony over it. One definition of good design could be that it creates a desire in the observer to step inside. This entrance draws us toward it; we wish we could recline on that balcony. The ground story of brick clings to the Queen Anne, but note again that, in the Colonial Revival, clapboard has substituted for shingles in the second story. We are fortunate to have views taken before and after Broderick's major redesign of the front of the house in 1909 (fig. 102). There is no question that the present appearance is more opulent and follows the owner's rising star; it is, furthermore, a sensitive extrapolation of the earlier version. The roof now has a slight

FIG. 101 The John Broderick house (1902). Broderick was the Secretary of the Central Manufacturing Committee at General Electric which was responsible for deciding what products the company would manufacture. He was a close friend of Steinmetz and the author of two books: Pulling Together which concerned labor-management relations, and Forty Years With General Electric.

flare that adds an elegant touch. The much larger porch has heavier columns which are not colonial but instead show the influence the Bungalow style. The original Federal fanlight over the front door has become the inner vestibule door. The craftsmanship that went into these homes is a persistent marvel, and the total integration of this renovation is truly remarkable. Present-day attempts to "improve" old buildings invariably look "tacked on."

The Peckham house (1903) further illustrates this now-vanished concern for craftsmanship and quality (fig. 103). W.H. Peckham, owner of the Peckham and Wolf Lumber Company, was astute enough to insist upon the finest workmanship in his own home. Legend has it that three years were required to accumulate the lumber for the interior, but it is unlikely that completion was delayed on this account (fig. 104). At no other time has such a variety of superior building materials been so readily available. Prosperity and the cheap transportation grid made it possible to employ Italian marbles, exotic woods, and elaborate brass fittings, all of which could be secured in any community through widely circulated catalogues. At no other time have people taken such an interest in construction or gone to such lengths to seek novelty and quality.

The second owner, from 1924 to 1940, was Myron F. Westover, who was the Secretary of the General Electric Company from 1894 to 1928. Westover was responsible for the adoption of a

FIG. 102 The Broderick house as it appears today. The photograph was taken shortly after major changes were made on 1909.

FIG. 103   *The W. H. Peckham house (1903),*
1350 Wendell Avenue, early view.

then-novel concept, the company-sponsored group life insurance plan. This plan not only accomplished much good for General Electric employees, but it also affected the thinking of other industry leaders who instituted similar programs. He was trained as an attorney in the Midwest, but concluded that the East, not the West, was the land of opportunity. He moved to Boston in 1886, where he met Charles A. Coffin and was employed as his secretary for the Thomson-Houston Electric Company, one of the companies that merged to form the General Electric Company. A friend had advised him to apply for the position, but Westover had been reluctant as the field did not appear promising! At the time of his retirement, he wrote, "I am very thankful to have lived in such a period, and to have had the privilege from a ring-side seat, to watch the panorama of unparalleled progress, the rapid growth of knowledge, and control of natural forces, their use in the industrial arts and their application to the welfare and happiness of humanity."

The Wooster B. Curtiss house (c. 1903), 1260 Stratford Road, shows again the Colonial Revival block design, but in this case the front elevation is completely asymmetrical (fig. 105). More than with any house so far, we can visualize the dynamic tension in the Colonial Revival style between Victorian asymmetry and Georgian symmetry. A round-arch window is included in the design on two counts. On the one hand, it is related to the Palladian window; on the other, its inclusion is a survival of a Victorian style in which an arch usually appeared somewhere in the composition. The entrance way is particularly well-designed with its neat little pediment and small oval light arranged over a bench or "settle" (fig. 106). Curtiss graduated from Tufts University with a degree in electri-

FIG. 104 The chestnut panelled hall and stairway in the Peckham house could have been ordered premade by machine or could have been custom made to meet individual specifications. Chestnut is superior to oak because it contains more resin and will not warp.

FIG. 105   The Wooster B. Curtiss house (c. 1903).

FIG. 106 *Entrance of the Curtiss house.*

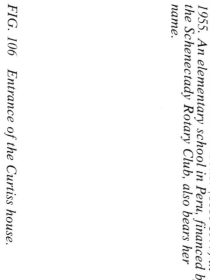

FIG. 107 Mrs. Jessie T. Zoller (1880-1977) in 1955. *An elementary school in Peru, financed by the Schenectady Rotary Club, also bears her name.*

FIG. 108 *The William C. Kitchin house (1904), 1196 Rugby Road.*

FIG. 109   William Kitchin house, detail.

FIG. 111   Georgian scrollwork of the Riley house.

FIG. 110 The John Riley house (1906).

cal engineering. At his death in 1924, he was supervisor of production at General Electric and assistant to vice-President Emmons.

Subsequently, Jessie T. Zoller lived in this home for several decades until her death in 1977. Mrs. Zoller, after whom Zoller Elementary School in Schenectady was named, served on the School Board from 1931 to 1958, never missing one of its 700 meetings. She was President of the Board after 1935, and she was also first woman President of the New York State School Board Association. She was recognized as being the driving force which made Schenectady's school system the envy of the rest of the state, and her efforts resulted in classes for the blind, the hospitalized, the mentally retarded, and those afflicted with cerebral palsy (fig. 107).

Similar to the Curtiss house, the William Kitchin house (1904) has a round arch, this time in the dormer (figs. 108, 109). The entire dormer has been turned into a small balcony—a marvelous treatment of that central dormer that we have seen on the Colonial Revival houses. Also, the dormer on the west side has been modified to surmount a full two-story bay window. Such extended bays were a high-style motif in the Victorian period. Atop the rock-faced masonry, porch piers are paired, Federal style colonnettes, which, in the true Federal, would be full-length.

The John Riley house (1906), 1175 Stratford Road, lacks the aggressive design of the Kitchin house. There appears little new here after the houses we have already considered. Yet, the house shows how the Colonial Revival style could be handled to create a quiet, stately design, lavish but subdued (fig. 110). We see the signature of the style in a fanlight Federal entrance used not over the door but on the vestibule enclosure, and we see Georgian scrollwork in the dormer (Fig. 111). Neither of these motifs has been used in places where it would have appeared in its parent period. For instance, these scroll decorations graced big gable ends, never porches or dormers as we have seen them in the Realty Plot. The colossal pilasters on the corners, as well as the porch columns,

FIG. 112 *The Alexander Vedder house (1907),*
1286 Wendell Avenue.

are extremely rich; and the modillioned eaves have been broadened to include symmetrically projecting bays on the second story.

The Wendell Avenue home of Judge Alexander M. Vedder (1907) is the last we shall consider in this chapter (fig. 112). All Colonial Revival designs include colonial elements which have been distorted in some way to create new effects. Here, we can see a round Federal porch with slender colonnettes, but the porch is much too large to be authentic, and the colonnettes are resting on piers of rock-faced masonry. All the windows are grouped in threes, an arrangement which repeats the wide front door with its two sidelights. For the architect, selecting a well-designed façade outweighed considerations of historical accuracy.

Judge Vedder served a total of thirty-five years in public life, first as District Attorney, for three years, and then as Judge in the City, County, and Surrogate Courts. In all those years he never suffered defeat at the polls, and none of his decisions were ever reversed by higher courts. Whether his domestic pronouncements went thirty-five years without successful appeal we cannot know, but Judge Vedder's home was designed like his courthouse so that, at work or play, he was constantly reminded of his heritage.

In this chapter we have seen how the spirit of Nationalism influenced architecture. The homes themselves were powerful patriotic statements, and the sense of "America the Beautiful" pervaded every aspect of daily life in a way that has no present parallel.

CHAPTER V

From Queen Anne to Colonial Revival

I have no reason to suppose that I am more curious than other people, but I confess I should like to see a person who is fairy down to the waist, but whose legs are mortal.

Iolanthe
W.S. Gilbert

We will now consider a group of hybrid designs falling between the Queen Anne and the Colonial Revival: in this respect, these homes incorporate some of the most instructive architecture in the Realty Plot. We saw that the Queen Anne style was popular before the Realty Plot was developed and that it clung until 1909. The Colonial Revival was introduced only shortly before the year 1900 and is seen here until 1912. The houses in this chapter, all built between 1902 and 1908, reflect their transitional status.

The earliest of these houses was, for over sixty years, the home of Dr. Ernst Alexanderson, famed for his pioneer work in television. Described by his friends as an absent-minded scientist who "couldn't open a can of soup," he was eulogized as an associate of Steinmetz and Marconi. He was General Electric's most prolific inventor, receiving a total of 322 patents during his forty-six years with the Research Laboratory, nearly one every seven weeks (fig. 114). Dr. Alexanderson, the son of a language professor, was born in Sweden and did his postgraduate work in Berlin. While there, he read Steinmetz's book *Alternating Current Phenomena* and was so impressed that he moved to Schenectady to work with the author. He took the company's Test Engineering course, and in 1904 he became a member of the engineering staff. Alexanderson's first assignment was to develop a high-frequency alternator that could produce a continuous radio transmission. At that time, radio consisted only of Morse code dots-and-dashes, transmitted intermittently by electric spark discharges. Professor Reginald Fessenden, a radio pioneer, asked the company if a high frequency, 100,000 cycles-per-second wave could be produced which would allow a continuous radio transmission. The concept was to produce a continuous carrier signal that could carry voice transmission, much as the telephone—in contrast to the telegraph—allowed voice transmission. The seemingly impossible task of developing a 100,000 cycle generator at a time when generators commonly operated at 60 cycles took Dr. Alexanderson two years.

On Christmas eve, 1906, the first radio broadcast took place from Brant Rock, Massachusetts. According to one account, "Early that evening wireless operators on ships within a radius of several hundred miles sprang to attention as they caught the call 'CQ, CQ' in Morse code. Was it a ship in distress? They listened eagerly, and to their amazement, heard a human voice coming from their instruments—someone speaking! Then a woman's voice rose in song. It was uncanny. Many of them called to the officers to come and listen; soon the wirless rooms were crowded." Further improvements to the alternator finally made possible transatlantic transmission. Its first important practical test was the delivery of President Wilson's ultimatum to Germany, October 20, 1918, which brought World War I to a close. At Wilson's behest, General Electric did not sell rights to the alternator to foreign interests (headed by Marconi, the "father of radio"); when this led to the formation of the Radio Corporation of America in 1919, Dr. Alexanderson became its Chief Engineer.

Later, he worked as a pioneer in the infant field of television. The first home reception of a televi-

90

FIG. 113 View of Wendell Avenue taken by
Charles Steinmetz on September 1, 1903, from
his balcony, Hillcroft, the home of H.W. Darling,
can be seen in the middle background; the
Anderson house, in the right background. This
photograph establishes the age of the Peckham
house, which can be seen under construction
in the right foreground. The cross street is
Avon Road.

FIG. 115   Alexanderson viewing television in his home in 1927.

FIG. 114   Ernst F.W. Alexanderson (1878-1975).

FIG. 116 The Alexanderson house (c. 1902),
1132 Adams Road.

sion program took place in the Adams Road home in 1927 (fig. 115). Though the techniques were crude by present standards, remarkable feats were accomplished. Transmissions of movies from Schenectady were received in Los Angeles, and in 1930 a public demonstration occurred at Proctor's Theater. As part of that broadcast from the General Electric laboratory, the theater orchestra was led by the conductor's image on a seven-foot screen.

Dr. Alexanderson purchased his home at 1132 Adams Road in 1911; from the price on the deed, it is evident that the house was standing at that time (figs. 116, 117). The house is present on the 1905 atlas, and city directories list "Edward B. and Elizabeth Clark, General Auditor, G.E. Co." as living there from 1902 to 1910. It appears that Clark neither owned nor built the house as the directory usually includes an "h" in the listing to denote a home owner. Finally, the deed to Dr. Alexanderson was granted by the Schenectady Realty Company, and there are no earlier recorded transactions involving the property. (If someone had purchased the property and built this house, their name would appear on the deed.) This house is another constructed by the Realty Company, posing the interesting, unanswered question of why the house was built.

Much of the house is Queen Anne. The broad Richardsonian windows and the wrap-around porch are typical of the style. There is an overall asymmetry, and a two-story polygonal bay with a candlesnuffer top is integrated into the roof line. Taken individually, its features are Queen Anne, and yet the effect is not Queen Anne at all. Clapboards are used as siding, evoking the Colonial Revival. Then, too, there is the Georgian scrollwork in the porch pediment, typical for the Colonial Revival. The delicately fluted porch columns would only need to be paired to fit nicely on the grander porches of the preceding chapter. Paired brackets under the eaves in the gable come from the Italianate Victorian period, a style which predates the Queen Anne. The house looks a bit like a farmhouse of the 1880's, and it would appear to be the creation of a skilled, older carpenter. An

FIG. 117 Porch detail, Alexanderson house.

94

FIG. 118 *The Austin Liecty house (c. 1902). The owner was the president and publisher of the Schenectady Gazette from 1920 to 1945. He was a charter member of the Associated Press.*

FIG. 119 *Portion of the west façade of the Liecty house.*

apt description of the total effect is "quaint." As Dr. Alexanderson was not give to material excess, this diminutive house nestled on Adams Road suited him well.

The Austin Liecty house (c. 1902), 3 Douglas Road, is a more typical example of the transitional architecture in the Realty Plot (fig. 118). The house has an asymmetrical plan that cannot be called Colonial Revival. There are numerous polygonal bays, and the fancy brackets under the overhanging dormers are completely Victorian. A gambrel (double-pitched) roof may lend a Dutch colonial inflection, but as we shall see in a later chapter, this roof design was a standard one for the Queen Anne. Also visible are broad, multipaned above, and a wrap-around porch; the house even has some shingle work in the street gable end. Yet, imbedded in this shingle work is a large Palladian window, albeit oddly proportioned. We must recall that architects sought to vary designs so that they would not be accused of plagiarism. A tall, central, rectangular window flanked by two lower windows on the west façade might be termed a "false" Palladian window (fig. 119). The trim under this window is the classical baroque scrollwork we have seen elsewhere. The house is entirely clapboarded save for the one area of shingles noted above. So, although the house has as great an asymmetry as any classified as Queen Anne, the feeling of the house is that of the Colonial Revival period because of the clever ways the architect has strategically utilized elements of the later style.

The J.H. Shugg house (1904), 1191 Stratford Road, is more symmetrical and thus steps farther toward the Colonial Revival, but here again the initial impression is deceptive; for while the front porch, with its Federal style balustrade and pedimented porch entrance, is certainly Colonial Revival, the vertical oval window on the second story belongs with either Queen Anne or Colonial Revival (fig. 120). Meanwhile, the front entrance has no colonial reference, being an original adaptation of standard interior paneling to the exterior of the house, and the building is shingled in the

FIG. 120   *The Shugg house (1904).*

FIG. 121   *Entrance of the Shugg house.*

FIG. 123 Interior of Lyon's Drug Store at 335 State Street. The date of the photograph is unknown.

FIG. 122 Richardsonian style recessed window, Shugg house.

Queen Anne manner (fig. 121). The house also does not have a hipped roof. Perhaps the fusion of styles is best exemplified by the bold window high in the gable (fig. 122). That folding in of the shingles to a recessed window is drawn straight from Richardson, but here it is topped with a fancy, classical scroll pediment.

The house across the street was built for J. Alexander Lyon, who operated Lyon's drug store on State Street (figs. 123, 124). The house should remind one of the McDermott house on Wendell Avenue (fig. 26). Here again the original porch has been removed, and the double-leafed door replaced by a proper Federal door. Picture this house with a Victorian entrance, wrap-around porch, red brick and rock-faced masonry, and the bulging bay window. There is really nothing to remove it from the Queen Anne, but the overall design has a Colonial Revival rectangular plan with hipped roof and central dormer. Since 1938, this

has been the residence of Mr. and Mrs. Harold Blodgett. Mr. Blodgett, known as the "dean of Schenectady's attorneys," was noted for his dramatic summations at the conclusion of trial testimony. Wreathing his wry wit in cigar smoke, he was a familiar figure on State Street during his sixty-six years of active practice (fig. 125). When the Blodgetts purchased the house, however, they were newcomers who upset some residents because Mrs. Blodgett did her own yard work. During the first winter, she recalls, a neighbor invited her in for coffee after she had been shoveling snow. She was glad the Blodgetts had moved in, the neighbor confided: "I always wanted to shovel myself, but didn't have the courage to do it."

FIG. 124 The J.A. Lyon house (c. 1904), 1186 Stratford Road. Under the influence of the Colonial Revival style, the prominent tower seen on the McDermott house has retreated into the body of this house to become a bulging two-story bay window.

FIG. 125 Harold Blodgett (1890-1979).

Two houses included in this chapter represent unpretentious creations that graft the symmetry of the Colonial Revival style onto the vernacular Queen Anne (figs. 126-128). These probably represent the product either of a contractor or of a junior architect of a large firm. The circumstances under which George Whittlesey built on Nott Street are not known. Mr. Whittlesey never lived in the house, and in 1911 he commissioned a finer dwelling on Lowell Road. Maxwell Day, who was granted thirteen patents, was an engineer in the Marine department at General Electric best known for his work applying electricity to such auxilliary marine functions as the ventilating of ships, the

FIG. 127 The Maxwell Day house (1904), 11½ Rugby Road.

FIG. 128 The Maxwell Day house.

FIG. 126 The George Whittlesey house (1905), 1014 Nott Street.

turning of gun turrets, and the hoisting of ammunition. The Whittlesey house is a simple block using a jerkin-headed gable on each end (fig. 126). This roof style came out of the medieval European tradition and began appearing in American architecture in the 1870's. There are few architectural details, and the house derives most of its artistry from simple symmetry. The Day house retains Queen Anne styling with the second story skirting out over the first. The upper and lower stories have the characteristic Queen Anne contrast of surface, but as part of the hybrid design, the first story is clapboard (figs. 127, 128). In spite of the polygonal bay on the left, the design is

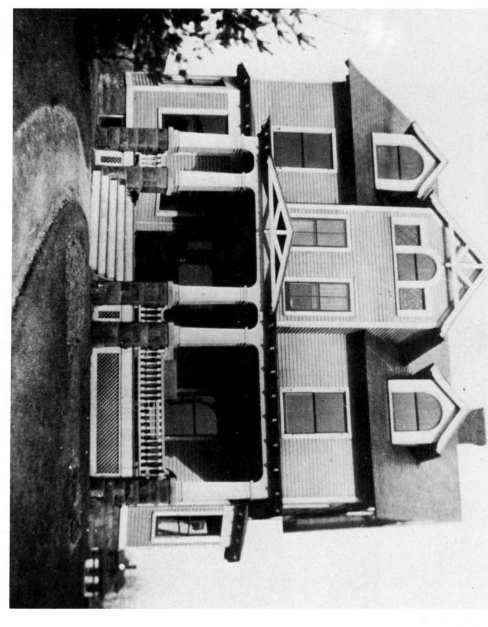

FIG. 129 The Hanson house (1906), 1262 Lowell Road, early photograph.

fairly symmetrical. A vertical oval window is the single "extra" which enriches the façade. In Chapter III we considered houses built around 1901 in a vernacular Queen Anne tradition. Here we see how the high-style Colonial Revival was beginning to affect vernacular construction in houses built a few years later.

H.A. Hanson's house was financed by his brother Willis T. Hanson, who owned the Hanson Drug Company. The house shows marked evolution toward the Colonial Revival as there is overall symmetry in spite of the polygonal bay on the left (fig. 129). The Palladian window in the central tower has a squattier appearance than a true Georgian Palladian window, and the round-arched windows in the dormers reflect the arch in the Palladian window. (This "depressed" version of the Palladian window became the standard for such windows in the Colonial Revival period.) The tower is a vestige from the Queen Anne period when towers were considered mandatory components of the design, but while a Queen Anne tower is always placed at one corner, here it is located in the center to fit the dictates of Colonial Revival symmetry. This is a fascinating example of how this architect served two masters! The purely decorative "stickwork" in the gable is from the Victorian era.

The Oliver Kline house (1908), 1212 Rugby Road, was executed by the same architect, Cortland Van Rensselaer; both houses show the architect's interest in multigable designs (fig. 130). Of the two, the Kline house makes a more powerful statement. The Federal doorway is surmounted by a polygonal bay, and high in the gable is an arch over a recessed bank of windows. There is a wonderful rhythm to the curves of the balustrade across the porch which reflect the curve of the fanlight over the door and the arch in the gable. A central axis of symmetry rises through the doorway to the great descending gable, but beyond that there is a play of asymmetrical elements across the center axis to create a dynamic balance. There are two Palladian windows on the west side with stained glass in the central panel of one.

FIG. 130   *The Oliver S. Kline house (1908),*
1212 Rugby Road.

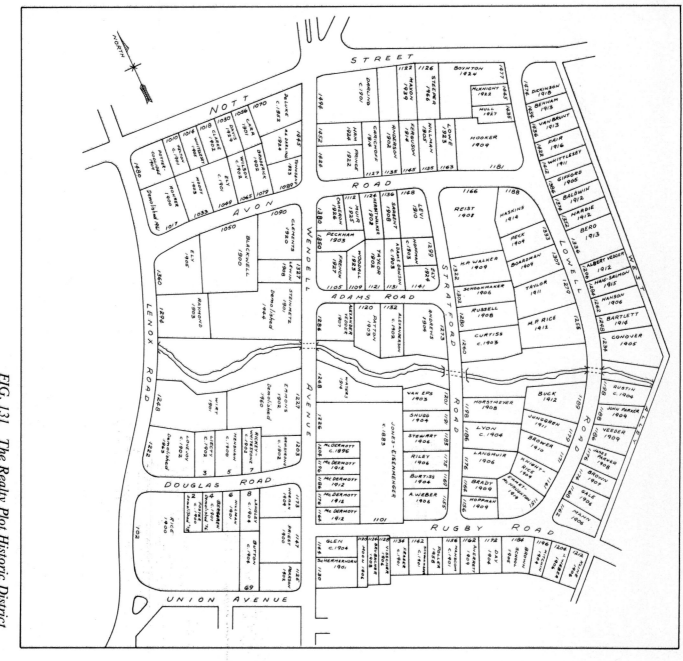

FIG. 131 The Realty Plot Historic District showing owners and dates of construction. The lot shapes are semischematic in some instances.

102

CHAPTER VI

The Colonial Imitation Style

According to an oral tradition, the Herbert C. Wirt house (1901), 1248 Lenox Road, was constructed as a replica of the John Hancock house (figs. 132-135). How close is the resemblance to John Hancock's house, and why did Mr. Wirt choose to emulate his taste? Fascinating tidbits of conjecture were unearthed when these questions were investigated. John Hancock's house was actually built by his Uncle Thomas in 1736 on Beacon Hill in Boston, adjoining the Boston Common (fig. 136). After John Hancock's death, the surrounding property was gradually sold, and the house was demolished in 1863 following last minute efforts to save it. A replica, however, was constructed for the Columbian Exposition in Chicago in 1893. We have previously noted the importance of this exposition in advancing the acceptance of the "Old Colonial" style. Further, in 1894, a book by Samuel Drake entitled *Our Colonial Homes* appeared. The cover of the book showed an outline of the Hancock Mansion, a picture of the house served as the frontispiece, and "The Hancock Mansion" was the first chapter of the book. Wrote Mr. Drake: "Our architects, those indefatigable purveyors to public caprice, after ransacking the whole earth, in search of novelty, wearied with turning all the old orders upside down and inside out, suddenly discovered that the Colonial residences of their own country have some merit. Old Colonial is at present the only proper style for a country house." So we may speculate that Wirt or his architect saw this house in Chicago or read Drake's book. But in the end, the Victorian impulse of the Colonial Revival car-

ried the day. The gambrel roof, the double chimneys at either end, and the balustrade across the roof are the only features common to the Hancock house. Elsewhere, the characteristic mixing of styles is expressed—for instance, in the wedding of the triangular, Georgian pediment over the projecting center of the house with a one-story, curved Federal porch.

In 1906, the house was puchased by Samuel Ferguson, a pioneer in the establishment of a power exchange system between utility companies. At the time of his death in 1950, he was the chairman of the board of directors of two power companies. The concept that utility companies should pool their generating capacities ultimately led to the present vast power grids that radiate from such places as Niagara Falls and Grand Coulee Dam.

We have noted the incompatibility of rationalistic, symmetrical, Georgian architecture with picturesque, asymmetrical Queen Anne, and in the preceding two chapters, we examined the product of the fusion of these two philosophies into the eclectic Colonial Revival style. Further, we observed that the evolution of the Colonial Revival gained impetus from the economic and political climate of the time as well as from the increasing number of trained architects who had spent a great many classroom hours studying and copying classical models. Purists, however, were bothered by the inaccuracies and excesses of the style. While we have noted with appreciation the juxtaposition of Georgian, Federal, and Greek Revival in one building, designers early in this century found such

FIG. 132 The Wirt house (1901) by Jones
Newball of Boston.

FIG. 133 *Early photograph of the dining room of the Wirt house.*

FIG. 135 *H.C. Wirt (1867-1919) was an inventor and protégé of E.W. Rice. He joined the General Electric Company in 1893 as Engineer of the Supply Department, where he made important improvements in the design and manufacture of wiring supply devices. In 1906, with a number of New England capitalists, he left Schenectady to form the Wirt Electric Company in Burrage, Massachusetts, a venture which did not prove successful.*

FIG. 134 *Hall, Herbert C. Wirt house.*

FIG. 136 Woodcut of the John Hancock house (1736), Boston, Massachusetts.

[8]Mr. Kettlewell and I discussed this term at length, for the word "imitation" may strike some as derogatory. Unfortunately, other terms used to describe these houses—such as "Period House," "Colonial style," or "Colonial Revival"—are not accurate. Thus, for this book, "Imitation" will remain the sincerest form of flattery.

poetic license objectionable. Graduate architects emerged who were trained and determined to go beyond the mere adaptation of colonial motifs to a true reproduction of the earlier designs. Surely, they said, these copies of early American houses would be a truly "American" style.

We will call houses cast in this mold "Colonial Imitation" style. The term is not meant to imply the exact appearance of the final product, as few of the houses built in this style exactly duplicate colonial models; instead, it is meant to describe the intent of the owner and architect.[8] In number, these represent the majority of the later houses in the Realty Plot. In part, this is due to the immense popularity of the style; in part, to the nature of the Realty Plot. Houses built in this style represented and continue to represent an ideal of taste and elegance. There were other building styles, but for the city home of a prominent citizen, the Colonial Imitation was the "appropriate" choice. The Wirt house has been included as a harbinger of the Colonial Imitation style.

To examine the style further, we now turn to much later examples which most closely approximate correct copies inspired by the colonial period. The Knight-Rice house (1909), 1161 Lowell Road, is a "five-bay" colonial—meaning that there are five windows or openings on each floor (fig. 137). With the exception of a screened porch on the left side, the house is entirely symmetrical. The house has such exclusively Federal detailing as a fanlight over the door, arched windows in the dormers, and twelve-pane windows. These windows tell us much about the style. We have noted again and again the Richardsonian windows, multipaned above with a large single pane below; now, for the first time, we see an accurate Colonial arrangement which uses small panes throughout. The use of twelve-pane windows on the Knight-Rice house traces to the post-Revolutionary or Federal period. Prior to the Revolution, windows usually were constructed with more than twelve panes, in part because of the costliness of larger panes of glass. Because the house has lost any reference to the earlier Georgian style, it might

FIG. 137 *The Knight-Rice house (1909) repre-*
sents an attempt to build a museum-quality
replica of a Federal style house.

107

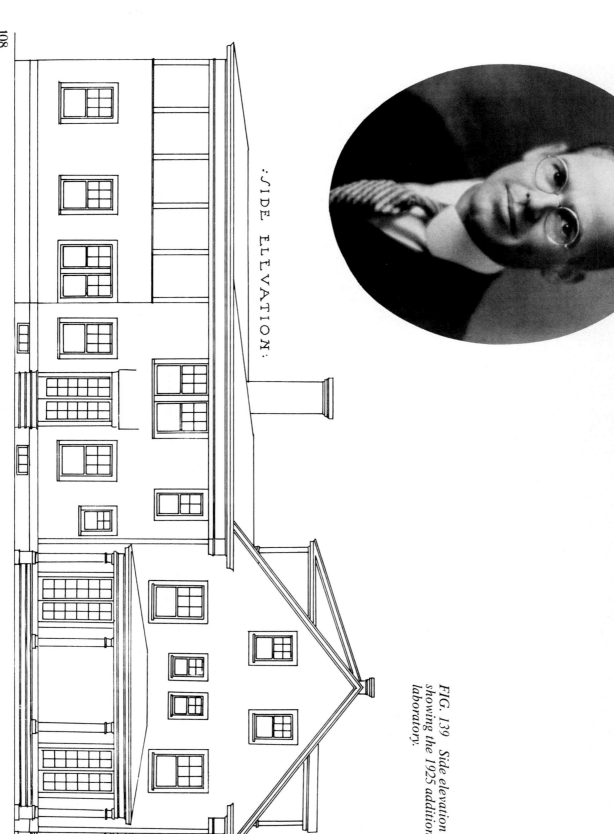

:SIDE ELEVATION:

FIG. 138 Chester W. Rice (1888-1951).

FIG. 139 Side elevation by W.T.B. Mynderse showing the 1925 addition which includes the laboratory.

better be designated as "Federal Imitation" than Colonial Imitation since, by any strict definition, "Colonial" would be pre-Revolutionary. The builders, however, were themselves somewhat confused as to what had been built in colonial days; if we define the Colonial Imitation style by the intent of the builders, then our term is an acceptable one.

Charles Knight, an employee of the American Locomotive Company was the house's first owner. The second, from 1917 to 1968, was Chester W. Rice (fig. 138). Chester Rice, son of E.W. Rice (fig.29), graduated from Harvard University in 1911 with a Masters degree in Electrical Engineering. Rice, not an early riser, preferred to work by himself late into the night. To accommodate his inventive genius, General Electric built a laboratory for him in his home which included a cement pier sunk eighteen feet into bedrock to insulate his sensitive equipment from the buffeting of trolleys (fig. 139). It is tempting to speculate that the company bowed to his wishes because of his illustrious father, but this is probably not the case: other scientists, such as Steinmetz, also worked at home. Equipment for research was not as complex as it is today; Edison's East Orange laboratory was really only a barn. The term "inventor" had more currency in those times; it was not considered odd for a scientist to putter in solitude.

As with John Bellamy Taylor and Ernst Alexanderson, it is difficult to describe Chester Rice's many areas of research. In 1926 he was granted a patent for the detection of submarines through the use of sound (sonar), and later he developed the "Sonic Altimeter" for use in airplanes. The Rice-Kellogg radio loudspeaker (1924) was still in general use at the time of his death in 1951, and in 1950 he invented the Halogen Detector to detect the minutest leak in a gas container or pipeline. This last device has been widely used in testing refrigerators. Probably most interesting was his early work in radar in 1928. It is generally known that the first practical application of radar was during the Battle of Britain, but radar research had been going on in several countries throughout the 1920's and 1930's. Alexanderson had devel-

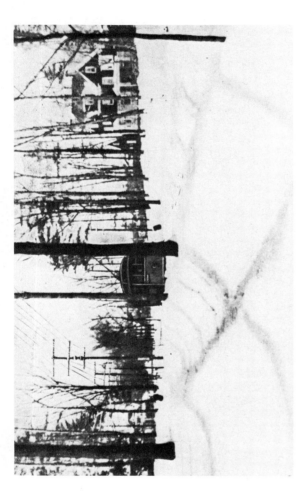

FIG. 140 *Postcard view of Rugby Road looking west showing the trolley Rice detected with his radar beam.*

oped a method for determining the altitude of an airplane by bouncing radio beams off the ground. Rice's Sonic Altimeter accomplished the same feat with sound. Rice took up Alexanderson's research; using very short radio waves he was able to detect a trolley car passing on Rugby Road from a window in his laboratory (fig. 140). Carrying this further, he moved his equipment to his roof and detected a small plane on its way to the Schenectady County Airport.

After Rice's death, his widow lived quietly on Lowell Road with her cook and housekeeper until 1968. Bespeaking a graciousness that has now been lost, the will provided that the domestic help would stay in the house until it was sold. This they did, living in the vacant house, polishing the brass, and lining closets and drawers until the day the new owners arrived.

Like the Knight-Rice house, the Anna Benham house (1913) is a complete expression of the Colonial Imitation style by the same architect, W.T.B. Mynderse (fig. 141). Here again we see Federal detailing within a five-bay design. The white lintels over the windows are a little thin, but similar lintels were characteristic in the Federal period. As with the previous example, a small one-story, colonnaded porch protects the entrance. The one-story porch was popularized in the Federal period, though the original version would be slightly shallower. Finally, the use of stucco is historically incorrect, but as we will discover, it was an increasingly popular siding material in the Realty Plot.

FIG. 141 The Anna Benham house (1913), 1454 Lowell Road. Mrs. Benham lived here quietly as a widow with her maid until 1925. Nothing is known of her except that she enjoyed giving tea parties for the neighborhood children.

The H.P. Walker house (1909), 1322 Stratford Road, is constructed of brick laid in Flemish bond in the correct colonial fashion (figs. 142-144). Again, there are five bays across the front, and here we see exaggerated keystones in the window lintels—another Federal touch. The entrance has classic Federal proportions, but the absence of a porch places it at variance with the group we are discussing. One later owner was Ralston Reid, general manager of General Electric's advertising and sales operations in charge of promoting more than two thousand products. Under his direction the department expanded from its original Schenectady site into a nationwide organization.

The Louise Dryer French house (1927), 1105 Adams Road (fig. 145), is surfaced in wide "weatherboards" and not the narrower clapboards. Weatherboard siding has been popularly associated with colonial Dutch architecture; but, in fact, it was used throughout the Colonies wherever this wide lumber was available, so it was not uniquely Dutch. Weatherboarding became popular in the Colonial Imitation style of the 1920's and 1930's, but it was not used on earlier Colonial Revival homes. However, imitation weatherboarding in the form of aluminum siding is commonly and inappropriately being applied to Colonial Revival buildings today.

The projecting porch has typical Federal paired colonnettes. What originally inspired these small porches was that, in the winter, a hard knock on the front door would bring all the snow from the roof down onto the visitor. That low arch in the pediment of the porch, repeating the arch over the doorway is common in Colonial Imitation designs but absent in the original version (fig. 146). In the door itself we see the classic proportioning of the panels with two tall panels surmounted by a short one.

The A.G. Darling house (1924) lacks the fidelity to the colonial style that we have so far seen (fig. 147). The house has no dormers as these were increasingly abandoned in the later years. This was due in part to increasing construction costs, in part to a "modern" striving for simple, "clean" lines. Modernism disapproved of the cluttered

FIG. 142   *The Henry P. Walker house (1909).*

FIG. 143 Entrance of the H.P. Walker house. Its diminutive proportions accurately duplicate the Federal style.

FIG. 144 The H.P. Walker house in May, 1910, prior to the addition of the south wing. Once more we see a porch attached to one side. Though they violate overall symmetry, they were popular in the Federal period.

FIG. 145 The French house (1927) is another example of the fully-developed Colonial Imitation style with its close approximation of an antique Federal design. Siding can tell much about the style of a house. Shingles are associated with the Queen Anne, clapboards with the Colonial Revival, and weatherboards (seen here) with the Colonial Imitation.

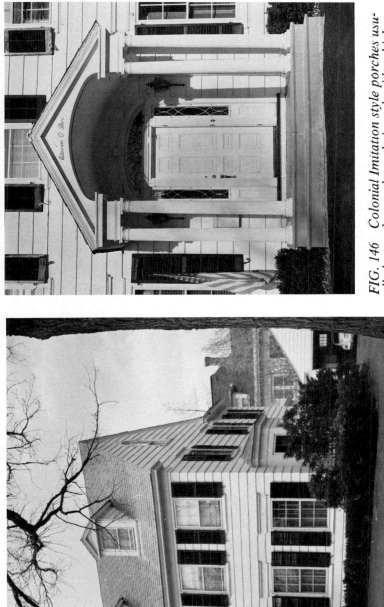

FIG. 146 Colonial Imitation style porches usually have a low arch on their underside which carries forward the outline of a fanlight window over the door. Such arches do not appear in the Federal period.

FIG. 147 *The A.G. Darling house (1924), 1445 Wendell Avenue.*

FIG. 148 *Alan Graeme Darling (1888-1968).*

effect of dormers interrupting the roof. Architects and patrons were losing interest in how exactly the house followed some earlier plan. It was sufficient that the house have a basic symmetry and be embellished with enough colonial detailing to establish the building as "Colonial." Thus, not only are the dormers absent, but the façade is not five-bay, and all the windows are not of uniform size. Nevertheless, this house falls into our grouping of houses in the Colonial Imitation style because of the obvious concern of the owner that the house be "authentic." A large number of items salvaged from older homes were used. The doorway with its fluted Corinthian columns came from an old farmhouse on Van Antwerp Road. The lock on

the front door was from the Van Voast house, formerly at the corner of Brandywine Avenue and Union Street. "H" and "L" hinges were Shaker-made, and hand-hewn beams came from demolished houses on lower State Street.

An eminent engineer, Alan Graeme Darling was the son of H.W. Darling, Treasurer of the General Electric Company. In 1955 he was honored by the American Institute of Electrical Engineers with a fellowship for "his contribution toward improving efficiency and operation of large industrial power-generating systems." During World War I he was on loan from the General Electric Company to the U.S. Fuel Administration to serve on the Coal Conservation Commission, and in World War II he was

FIG. 149   *The Charles McKnight house (1922).*

FIG. 150 *Detail of the McKnight house (1922) includes medieval protrusion of the second story over the first with decorative drops.*

FIG. 151 *The Albert Hull house (1927), 1435 Lowell Road. Shutters on the ground floor have half-moon silhouettes; the second floor shutters have diamonds. Elsewhere in the Realty Plot, pine trees and other designs can be found in the shutters. These silhouettes originate in this period.*

connected with the Manhattan Project (fig. 148).

The Colonial Imitation style was codified by decorating services provided by such organizations as the Home Builder's Service Bureau, operated by the *House Beautiful* magazine. By offering standardized plans of "type" houses which were "pleasing architecturally, economical in arrangement, and of a superior character," the magazine endeavored to "raise the standard of small houses in this country." In addition, it gave advice on interior decoration, furnishings, plantings, and designing grades and walks: it also offered complete landscape designs. Finally, a staff of architects would modify standard plans to the individual requirements of owners. (All this, incidentally, was accomplished by mail!) Coincidentally, two houses built side by side on Lowell Road were rendered from these plans.

Like the A.G. Darling house, the Charles McKnight house (1922), 1445 Lowell Road, with three bays and a gambrel roof, does not fit the pattern so far discussed (fig. 149). Overhanging the first story, the second features the same medieval pendants on the corners present on the House of the Seven Gables (fig. 150). This is not, as we would expect, a five-bay house; furthermore, wings extend from each side of the house. Nevertheless, the doorway is classically Federal and similar to the Walker house (fig. 143). Actually the architect for *House Beautiful* has constructed an extended fantasy. If authentically Colonial, this house would have been built in the medieval tradition in the early 1700's. Later, additions to the sides and the insertion of a Federal doorway would have been added to enlarge the house for a growing family and to make it more fashionable. In the Federal period such a hybrid house would have been a common occurrence. It is to this hybrid quality that the architect alludes. He has retained the shingled siding common in the Connecticut valley—the siding, adopted by Richardson to provide a Colonial effect, which was subsequently assimilated into the Queen Anne style.

The Hull house (1927), the other *House Beautiful* design, better fits the Colonial Imitation mold

FIG. 152   *This view of the entrance was used on Christmas cards in 1938.*

FIG. 153   Dr. Albert Hull (1880-1966) in his living room.

(fig. 151). Dr. Hull was an active participant in every phase of the design; he roamed the city, taking snapshots of houses to help him visualize how his finished house might appear. Only a fraction of his correspondence with the Home Builder's Service Bureau remains, but in one letter, dated April 28, 1927, he listed thirteen criticisms and added, "I am tired of objecting. Obviously, if I could tell you all the things that are wrong and how to right them, I could design my own house without your help." By July 6, 1927, however, he could report that "the new . . . plans are entirely satisfactory" and work began.

The windows in the five bays are somewhat squat for true Colonial windows, and shutters with cut-out silhouettes are original to the 1920's, but the overall effect is classic Colonial Imitation. There is a nicely done entrance in which the Federal fan is on the surface of the building while the doorway itself is recessed (fig. 152). It is an authentic and practical alternative solution to the problem of snow sliding off the roof. When a visitor heard movement overhead, he could jump into the recess to avoid the avalanche. Nevertheless, the design is not quite accurate because recessed doorways only became common in the later Greek Revival period.

Dr. Albert Hull died in 1966, at age of 85, after working over fifty years at the General Electric Research Laboratory. He was its Assistant Director from 1928 to 1949. His main area of expertise was in the field of vacuum tubes, the cornerstone of electronics until the development of the transistor. The workings of the screen-grid-tube, one of his inventions, should be familiar to anyone still versed in high school physics, for this tube forms the basis of radio and television receivers. An early and far-reaching invention was the magnetron, a vacuum tube in which the current is controlled by a magnetic field. The magnetron lay dormant until it proved to be an ideal generator of microwaves for radar transmitters as well as a powerful generator of high frequency waves for "jamming radar." During World War II, a continuing race to develop better radar or countermeasures to nullify it was carried out on both sides. Dr. Hull headed the laboratory's efforts in this field. His inventive genius saved thousands of American lives. For example, in one week in the fall of 1944, Hull's group produced a special set of magnetrons to jam a newly developed Japanese low-frequency radar. As a result of his wartime contributions, he was awarded both the Presidential Certificate of Merit and the U.S. Army's Decoration for Distinguished Civilian Service (fig. 153).

The Nott street home of Richard P. Davis (1929) wsa built by John F. Horman (fig. 183) and was given by him to his daughter and son-in-law at the time of their marriage (figs. 154, 155). Quartered windows in the gable ends were a standard feature of American architecture: they appeared during the Georgian period and flourished in the Federal before they were abandoned during the Greek Revival. The tapered chimney fits nicely with the building, but the picturesque quality it lends is historically inaccurate. First, true period chimneys were built into the building so that more of their heat would be retained on the inside. (This left a flat gable end when the building was viewed from outside.) But modern building codes discouraged this practice due to the risk of fire. Second, a tapered chimney would only be correct in the medleval style. Although tapering not only strengthens the chimney but also improves its function by creating a better draft, the tapered appearance was not desired by Federal builders who insisted upon straight lines (fig. 156). This chimney shows how the Colonial Imitation at once attempted to copy the past while at the same added its own stamp of individuality.

The Alexander Cameron house (1926), 1380 Wendell Avenue, is unique in the Realty Plot as it is the only house built after a Spanish Colonial style (figs. 157, 158). When we initially discussed the architectural heritage of the country, we noted that the many regional variations were blurred in the emerging revival styles. This was essentially because most people identified Colonial times with pre-Revolutionary New England or Williamsburg. Yet there were some regional variations in the

FIG. 154 *The Richard Davis house (1929), 1030 Nott Street, is similar to the Hull house, even in such details as the recessed entrance.*

FIG. 155 Entrance of the Davis house.

FIG. 156 West elevation of the Davis house, showing quartered windows and tapered chimney.

120

FIG. 157   *The Alexander Cameron house (1926), 1380 Wendell Avenue.*

expression of the Colonial Imitation style. The houses in the Realty Plot are essentially Federal, while those built during the same period on Monument Avenue in Richmond, Virginia, are Georgian (fig. 159). The Georgian tradition was undoubtedly stronger there (its numerous Georgian-style plantations can still be visited). For those living in the American Southwest, the architecture of the Spanish mission provided a model for a Spanish Colonial style. But a small yet significant number of such Spanish Colonial designs are scattered throughout the Northeast. We can only speculate why owners chose this style. The Cameron house would be remarkable in any locale, but it is singu-

lar amidst our banks of snow on a January day. Maybe Mr. Cameron had worked in the South, or maybe he was captivated by a movie or a magazine.⁹ As one approaches the front door (in July, not January!) the illusion of El Dorado is striking (fig. 160).

The house is not a true imitation of the Spanish Colonial style because it is too artfully designed. A true Spanish Colonial, with its blend of baroque ornamentation and Pueblo Indian construction, lacks the studied design of this house. Consider its three planes: the projecting central section, the slightly recessed wing on the right, and the deeper recess of the wing on the left. Windows in the left wing are set slightly lower than those in the right wing. The arched pair of windows over the entrance

have a column separating them, but only the capitals of the columns flank the windows (fig. 160). Presumably the architect studied this carefully before deciding that only one complete column should be used. The shutters undoubtedly copy some Spanish model. They have been hung using larger hinges on the top; this achieves twin purposes. First, gravity will open the shutters when they are unhooked and will help hold them in that position. Second, the slight sag of the shutter lends a subtle informality to the composition. The surface stucco work is "rough cast," i.e., the plaster has been literally thrown in trowelfuls at the walls. This technique is not only difficult to duplicate but also adds expense due to the amount of wasted material.

Across the street from the Cameron house

⁹*Maybe this eclecticism is not incomprehensible. How many houses are being built in a "Cape Cod" style in Montana?*

FIG. 158 The Cameron house.

stands the home of David Chandler Prince (figs. 161, 162). This house combines the steep roof and asymmetrical window openings of the medieval style with other elements drawn from the Georgian style, such as the balanced placement of two large chimneys. An English source for the design is suggested by the plaster exterior, the quoining on the corners, and the carved lintel over the door. This house is an adaptation of an English cottage which would have been the home of a prosperous English farmer in the seventeenth or eighteenth century. Like the Spanish Colonial nearby, this house idealizes an architectural style prevalent during our colonial days, though not a style seen in this area. Also like the Spanish Colonial, this house is really too artfully designed to replicate the earlier period. The window openings are carefully arranged across the façade, and the wren house atop the garage cleverly balances the chimneys. The garage itself is recessed and lower than the main body so that it will not detract from the overall effect (fig. 163).

D.C. Prince was a staff engineer with the Research Laboratory and an assistant to Dr. Alexanderson. Among his ninety-eight patents was the giant oil circuit breakers installed in Boulder Dam in 1934 which operated at record-breaking voltages. Later, he became a vice-president of General Electric and head of the General Engineering and Consulting Laboratory. He had little interest in the construction of the house, according to his granddaughter, and left this "mundane activity" to his wife. Mrs. Prince came from a family of architects, and so she wisely selected Thomas Harlan Ellet who had recently won the *Prix de Rome*. He is best known for the American Military Chapel and Cemetery at Thiaucourt, France, the Cosmopolitan Club in New York City, and a large number of post offices. Ellet in turn selected an aspiring friend, Paul Manship, to carve the lintel over the front door (fig. 164). Manship later achieved renown as a sculptor; his inventory includes the *Prometheus* statue in Rockefeller Center (fig. 165).

FIG. 160 *Central section of the Cameron house. Traditional to the Spanish Colonial and to the Colonial Imitation, a great deal of attention has been devoted to the doorway. The twisted columns on the shallow porch are typically Spanish Baroque as is the multipaneled door.*

FIG. 159 *The McGuire-Warthen house (1925), by Baskerville and Lambert, on Monument Avenue, Richmond, Virginia, is a Georgian style, Colonial Imitation design.*

Thus far we have looked at houses that closely copy colonial models. This we have done so that we can now better appreciate how other Colonial Imitation style houses in the Realty Plot deviate from being true replicas. There are two basic reasons why the Colonial Imitation style deviates from the Colonial style it mimics. First, many houses were designed by older architects who had worked in the Queen Anne and Colonial Revival style. Fashions changed, and to attract clients, these architects changed also, but their designs retained elements of the older styles. Not wanting to imitate the past slavishly, the architect included only enough "Old Colonial" to appease his client. The houses in this category show us a fascinating fusion

FIG. 161 *The D.C. Prince house (1922), 1424 Wendell Avenue, was featured in the October, 1926, issue of Garden and Home Builder. This photograph and the one following appeared in the magazine.*

FIG. 162   Dining room of the D.C. Prince house.

125

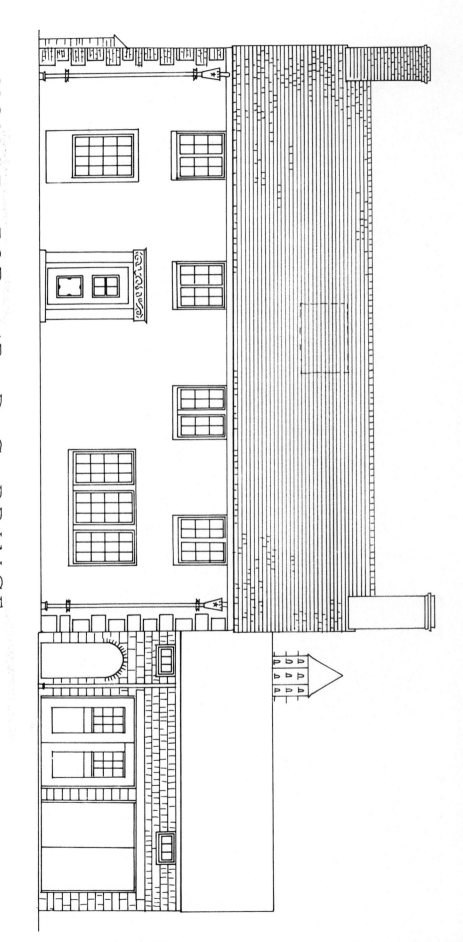

· H O U S E · F O R · M R · D · C · P R I N C E ·
· S C H E N E C T A D Y · N E W · Y O R K ·

FIG. 163   Front elevation of the Prince house by Thomas Harlan Ellet. The small-sized openings of the bird house over the garage identify it as a wren house. We can only speculate why the plan is a mirror image of the final product.

FIG. 165 *Prometheus by Paul Manship.*

FIG. 164 *Lintel by Paul Manship over the entrance of the Prince house.*

of the Colonial Revival or Bungalow style with Colonial Imitation. Second, the ideal of the Colonial Imitation style was to revive the clean, simple symmetry of colonial days. This end could be achieved short of board-by-board replication. Further, clients, especially the highly educated scientists of the Realty Plot, may have taken some control in the design. They might specify that the houses be "Colonial," but after some Colonial effects had been included in a doorway, they might then insist upon the addition of a window here or a dormer there. The "livability" of the house was beginning to take precedence over the design system. The houses in this group, to which we now turn our attention, are remarkably alike, but

they contrast sharply with a true Federal style design. All of these houses share in common a three-bay front instead of an authentic five-bay. Further, the windows in each bay are invariably broad, as the owners were unwilling to sacrifice the convenience of the large window which had been introduced in the Queen Anne period. If the house has dormers, they are three in number and line up with the windows below to create an intense symmetry exceeding that of the authentic Federal or Georgian periods. Finally, many of these houses are covered in stucco. Stucco comes from the English building tradition and was little used in this country in colonial times. (This connection will be discussed in Chapter X.) However, changing fashion was making its plain, flat, streamlined appearance desirable in a reaction to the ornamentation of the Victorian period. Stucco reduces

FIG. 166 Christmas, 1905, at 1273 Stratford Road. The fireplace shows beautiful Federal detailing of garlands and swags. The Indian artifacts were accumulated by Col. Andrews, who is seen reclining on the left.

the surface of the building to a neutral plane, and we will increasingly see its use in the Realty Plot. The net effect is to decrease the visual impact of the building as a whole and to focus attention on isolated elements such as the entrance. This does have an authentic ring, for one goal of the Federal style was to present a refined façade, with ornamentation reserved for the doors and windows. This Colonial Imitation style, thus, is unique.

These houses deserve appreciation and preservation because people who faced such unsettling events as World War I and the subsequent dismantling of the European empires and the rise of American technological might were making individualistic statements about themselves in their houses. These houses, then, help us understand that era.

Col. James Andrews commanded the old Second Regiment of the New York National Guard, which was federalized as the 105th Infantry, 27th Division. He was awarded a Distinguished Service Medal for his valor with "Black Jack" Pershing in Mexico and in France during World War I (fig. 166). The Col. James Andrews house (1904), 1273 Stratford Road, with that low arch in the porch pediment we noted earlier, is an early example of the Colonial Imitation style (figs. 167, 168). The basic three-bay design is concealed somewhat by

FIG. 167 The Andrews house as it appeared shortly after the south wing was added in 1911. The second owner was W. Howard Wright who founded the Schenectady Varnish Company in 1906. When World War II made the supply of gums uncertain, the company diversified into synthetic resins. Known as the Schenectady Chemical Company since 1962, the company is an important economic force in the community.

FIG. 168   Early view of the Andrews house showing the original clapboard exterior. Note that the dormers do not quite line up with the windows below as they will in later houses of this genre.

an addition dating to 1911, and the present stucco, as an earlier photograph shows, is not original (fig. 168). In addition to aesthetic considerations, stucco supplied insulation and lowered maintenance; it was the aluminum siding of its day.

The D. Mathias Van Eps house adjacent to Col. Andrews's residence across the ravine was built in the Colonial Revival style in 1903 with a large porch across the front and a polygonal bay (fig. 169). However, in 1929, the house was "modernized" to its present appearance. The Colonial Revival portion of the house that survives is the Georgian hipped roof and the Palladian window in the dormer (fig. 170). No real attempt has been made to duplicate a colonial house, but the Colonial Imitation impulse has been expressed by a neutral plaster surface, a symmetrical three-bay façade, and a smaller porch with Federal colonnettes. This house, then, is a true hybrid of the Colonial Revival and Colonial Imitation Styles.

By the time of the building of the Arthur Bradt house at 1164 Stratford Road in 1909, the three-bay Colonial Imitation style had hit its stride and continued with little change over the next fifteen years (fig. 171). Compare the Bradt house to the much later John Ham house (1924), 1452 Wendell Avenue (fig. 172). The porches on the two are strikingly similar. In addition to carrying the curve of the fanlight forward into the porch, both have porch seats, or "settles," that were intended to evoke the Dutch heritage of the Mohawk valley. In the Ham house a pair of small windows has

FIG. 169   Early postcard view of Stratford Road. The camera is located at the ravine, facing south, and the original porch on the Van Eps house is barely visible on the right side of the photograph.

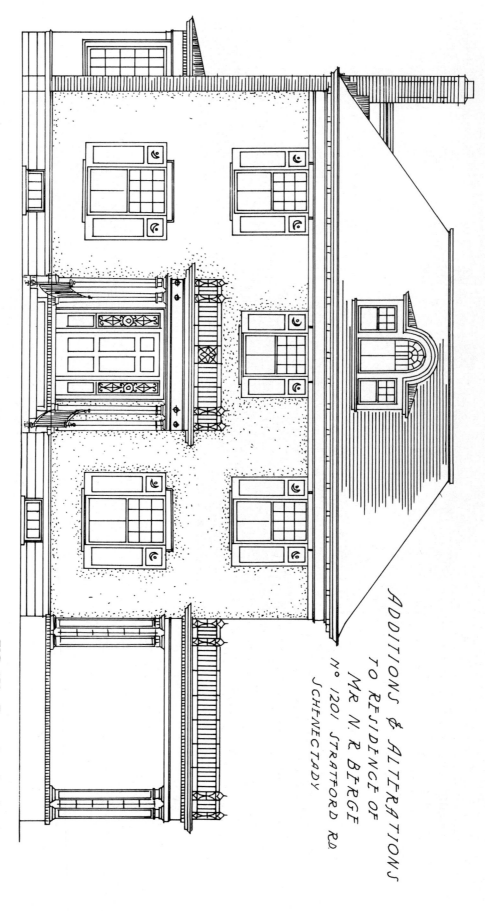

ADDITIONS & ALTERATIONS
TO RESIDENCE OF
MR N R BERGE
N° 1201 STRATFORD RD.
SCHENECTADY

FIG. 170   Front elevation drawing for the 1929
renovation of the Van Eps house.

FIG. 171   The Arthur Bradt house (1909).

been substituted for the central window of the second story. Symmetry is maintained, and we can assume that this rearrangement better suits the floor plan. The Ham house has no dormers, which represents a loosening of the style as well as an attempt to cut costs in the inflationary 1920's. This lack of dormers may presage more than an inflationary spiral, however. It is probable that the "Modern" trend in architecture to clean lines caused the dormer to be discarded.

The Edgar Dickinson house (1918), 1474 Lowell Road, is somewhat more elaborate than the previous examples (fig. 173). Although the three-bay format is retained, the ground floor has banks of three windows which become double windows in the upper story and culminate in single-windowed dormers.

Two houses of this group differ slightly from the others, and the differences may be related to the occupations of the owners. J.H. Clements, Jr., was the Secretary-Treasurer of the Peckham and Wolf Lumber Company. His house (1920) at 1090 Avon Road (fig. 174) is within sight of Mr. Peckham's Colonial Revival style home. As in Peckham's case, we can assume that Clements could appreciate quality construction. Thus, he used expensive, wide, weatherboard siding on his house. His porch is also slightly different from the others we have seen; its slender colonnettes and original fanlight treatment over the door are more academically correct (fig. 175). Probably because J.E. Lowe was in the construction business, his home at 1163 Avon Road (1923) was built with atypical materials (figs 176, 177). Neither the tile roof nor the orange brick is authentic to any colonial style, although they would not be out of place in the industrial buildings which were the forte of the Brown and Lowe Company.

FIG. 173   The Edgar Dickinson house (1918), 1474 Lowell Road.

FIG. 172   The John Ham house (1924). The term "stoop" actually comes from the Dutch "stoep," a term for a covered porch with seats such as this one. In English usage, the word now describes any small entrance stairway.

FIG. 174   The J.H. Clements house (1920), 1090 Avon Road.

FIG. 175   Entrance of the Clements house. Colonial Imitation entrances are more delicate than Colonial Revival entrances.

FIG. 176   The J.E. Lowe house (1923). The use of this color brick with a tile roof is practical but whimsical in this style, as the architect must have understood.

FIG. 178 The Arthur Buck house (1912), 1189 Lowell Road.

J. E. LOWE

FIG. 177 Caricature of J.E. Lowe from Schenectady Just For Fun. Evidently, Mr. Lowe enjoyed fishing.

FIG. 179   *The F.R. Schoonmaker house (1906).*

FIG. 180   *The F.R. Schoonmaker house, detail.*

The Arthur Buck house (1912), 1189 Lowell Road, is the archetypical example of the style (fig. 178). The house is far removed from a true Federal colonial house because the stucco is inaccurate, the three-bays are inaccurate, the lack of dormers is inaccurate, and the porch is inaccurate. Yet, to the average person in 1912 or today, the house embodies the colonial ideal. It is elegant; it is simple; it is American.

We are left with a group of dwellings that combine elements of the Colonial Revival style with the Colonial Imitation style. In them we will see none of the asymmetry that typified the Victorian era, but, on the other hand, there will be odd "inaccuracies" which bar the houses from unqualified inclusion in the Colonial Imitation style. For instance, the F.R. Schoonmaker house (1906), 1302 Stratford Road, has the symmetry of the Colonial Imitation overriding many elements taken from the Colonial Revival (fig. 179). Shingles have been used instead of clapboard or stucco, and the windows, though symmetrically disposed, are not in the five-bay mold. Instead, the placement of windows in pairs, as well as their single lower pane, identify them as belonging to the Queen Anne period. In the roof we see not a Federal style dormer but a continuous "shed" dormer which will become popular in the Bungalow style (fig. 180). The Henry Reist house (1908) likewise has shingles and a shed dormer; a full five bays are employed, but the house fails any precise comparison to the Federal style (fig. 181).

Henry Reist worked at General Electric as a design engineer in charge of developing electrical generators. When he began his work in the field, a 100-kilowatt generator was considered large, but under his guidance, performance steadily increased until, at his retirement in 1929, a 160,000-kilowatt generator was installed in the Fourteenth Street Station of the New York Edison Company. Mrs. Reist is well remembered as one of the Realty Plot's most gracious *grandes dames*. Well into the 1960's, in white gloves, she greeted new arrivals with her calling card and later invited them to tea.

FIG. 181 *The Henry Reist house (1908), 1166 Avon Road.*

FIG. 182 Early photograph of the John F.
Horman house (1909).

FIG. 183 *John F. Horman, civic and business leader (1860-1940).*

FIG. 184 *The furniture department of the H.S. Barney Company.*

A graduate with a degree in classics from Radcliffe College who also studied at the Sorbonne, she served as the second president of the local chapter of the American Association of University Women in 1923. Through her efforts art exhibits were first brought to Schenectady by that group, long before such exhibits were held at the Schenectady Museum. The Reists were keenly interested in botany, and their gardens were some of the most beautiful in the city. Mrs. Reist maintained this interest in her later years, and her many friends were delighted recipients of her flowers.

The Horman house (1909), 1173 Wendell Avenue, is a Colonial Revival style building so pronouncedly affecting Colonial Imitation symmetry that it seems more appropriate in this chapter than in the preceding one (fig. 182). It has more Greek Revival influence than any other house in the

Realty Plot. Witness the large, porch columns with their simple capitals, the simple pilasters used on the corners of the building, and the flat transom window over the door. Also observe the characteristic mixing of styles of the Colonial Revival in the Georgian roof composed of red slate, the hardest and finest of the many varieties of slate, and the anomalous Federal style door with two tall panels and one short panel.[10]

John F. Horman was born in Cincinnati in 1860 and operated a dry goods store there. In 1897 he became editor of a New York trade journal, the *Dry Goods Economist,* and in 1900 he came to Schenectady to work with Howland S. Barney. After Barney's death in 1904, Horman was General Manager, Treasurer and vice-President of the H.S. Barney Company (fig. 183). He operated the department store until 1935, when his son-in-law

became his successor. Barney's, known as "Schenectady's Greatest Store," flourished until the urban decline of the 1950's and 1960's led to its demise (fig. 184). To the store's credit, but hastening its fall, it maintained a policy of personalized service which regrettably became economically obsolete in the age of the computer checkout. For instance, the store maintained on file the measurements of fashion-conscious socialites who could order dresses by telephone for special occasions; the dresses were then delivered to the home for final fitting. Employees of the company were considered members of a large family. Horman was driven to work by a team each morning at six A.M. Sitting in his office near the rear entrance, he greeted each worker every morning with a handshake. On a cold day during the Depression, he observed that one clerk did not have a winter coat. He promptly

[10]*In the 1950's the house was owned for a time by a college fraternity. A fraternity brother relates that a well-placed bowling ball released from a car moving at high speed down Rugby Road will roll the length of the driveway and into the garage.*

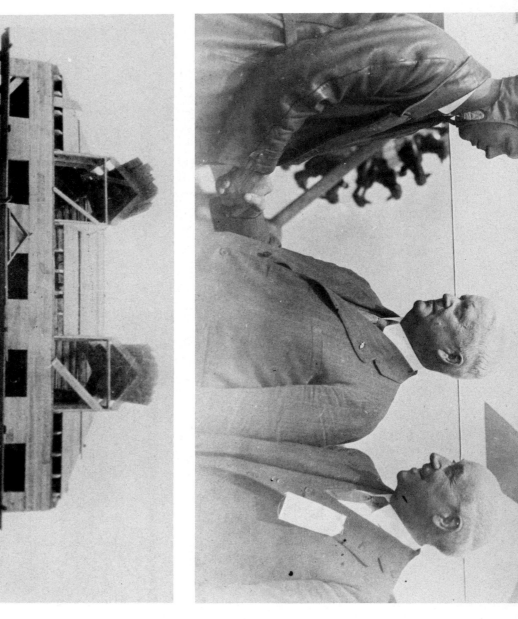

FIG. 185 Horman (right) greeting Charles Lindberg at the Schenectady County Airport on July 28, 1927. Lindberg landed here briefly in the Spirit of St. Louis while on a triumphant tour of 82 cities.

commanded his daughter to relinquish her own.

Horman was committed to community service, and during one long period, the Barney Company donated one percent of its earnings to welfare relief. He laid the cornerstone for the Union College Memorial Chapel. He was instrumental in the formation of the Chamber of Commerce and served as its first president from 1922 to 1926 (fig. 185). As a man of commerce and enterprise, he kept a sharp eye on any development related to his business. He is said to have engineered the great curve in the Western Gateway Bridge so that all traffic would spill out in front of his store instead of at the General Electric buildings.

In spite of his contributions to Schenectady and the fact that his house was pictured in the 1914 *Schenectadian* as one of the prominent residences of the city, it was deemed "worthless" and without architectural or historic significance by its owners in 1978 and was slated for demolition. Efforts to prevent this led to the formation of the present Realty Plot Historic District. Books such as this arise from an attempt to fill the void in some men's minds.

Built in 1914, the house of John F. Bartlett, patent attorney for General Electric, bears a striking resemblance to the Horman house (figs. 186, 187). As Mr. Bartlett followed the construction of the Horman house and approved of the design, this is no coincidence. Bartlett graduated as a Mechanical Engineer from Worcester Polytechnic Institute in 1892, and because he could find no other work, he labored for six months in an architect's office. Thus, he drew his own plans for his Lowell Road home and only utilized the services of an

FIG. 186 The Bartlett house under construction.

FIG. 187 *The John Bartlett house (1914), 1248
Lowell Road, early photograph.*

FIG. 188 *Mr. and Mrs. John F. Bartlett.*

architect during the construction phase. Since Bartlett's daughter has the ticket stub from his visit to the 1893 Columbian Exposition, he must have seen at first hand the Beaux Arts style that so influenced the architecture of the day. The house is slightly smaller than the Horman house, but the similarities are apparent. The last house in the Realty Plot constructed with a hipped roof in the Colonial Revival manner, it also has the same rough-cast plaster on a five-bay façade with simple white trim. Bartlett's Federal style entrance departs from Horman's design and is in keeping with the other Colonial Imitation style houses of this date.

Bartlett left the architect's office and moved to Washington, D.C., where he worked in the patent office while he attended law school at night. As the rooming house where he lived also included among its guests Harriet Ford, Henry's sister, Bartlett was introduced to the future industrialist before 1900, when Ford was considered a "crackpot." Bartlett's favorite lament in his later years was that he did not heed Ford's advice to invest in his automobile factory. While at the patent office, Bartlett met A.G. Davis (fig. 52), and he followed Davis to Schenectady upon graduation from law school. Bartlett loved gadgets, and his work at General Electric exposed him to novel ideas. The house contains a brass, automatic trip-switch in the frame of the closet door to turn on the closet light and a "burglar switch" in the master bedroom that will turn on all the lights on the first floor simultaneously (fig. 188).

It is interesting to compare the Garrett Veeder house (1909), 1186 Lowell Road, with the nearby Knight-Rice house as they were built in the same year. The Knight-Rice house is a close-to-perfect replica of a true Colonial style. Superficially, the Veeder house bears a close resemblance to it, but careful perusal reveals a number of "incorrect" features that tie it to the Colonial Revival style (fig. 189). First, consider the oak front door. Oak was infrequently used in colonial times because its extreme hardness and coarse grain made it difficult to achieve a smooth finish. Oak again became

FIG. 189 *The Garrett Veeder house (1909),*
1186 Lowell Road.

FIG. 190 Clapboard with decorative bead edge on the Veeder house.

popular in the late Victorian and Colonial Revival period (thus "golden oak" furniture), but it was dropped entirely in the Colonial Imitation style. Its use here associates the house with the earlier style. Second, the enclosed porch with the door projecting is also an original Colonial Revival creation. Third, there is characteristic over-embellishment. The dormers are loaded with ornaments that would not be found in the Federal or Georgian period, and the clapboard has a molded bead edge which was used in colonial times as an expensive extra (fig. 190).

The Albert J. Levi house (1910), 1148 Avon Road, has the Queen Anne style skirting of the upper story, profuse stained glass, a Victorian style entrance, and lavish ornamentation imposed upon a symmetrical Colonial Imitation frame (figs. 191, 192). There is much more Victorian feeling here, but the symmetry removes it from the Colonial Revival period. Albert Levi operated the Jonathan Levi Company after his father's death in 1906. Jonathan Levi had come to Schenectady from Germany in 1852 and opened a general store at 218 State Street. Gradually, the company grew and dropped its line of general merchandise to specialize in the grocery business. In his fifty-three years as a merchant in Schenectady, Jonathan Levi was connected with all the principal movements to advance Schenectady. Along with several other businessmen, he was instrumental in bringing the General Electric Company to the city. When Albert took control, he redirected the business to wholesale groceries. A few years later, he constructed his house in the Realty Plot. Levi resided here until his retirement in 1925 (fig. 193).

1279 Lowell Road was the second house built (1911) for John Bellamy Taylor in the Realty Plot (fig. 194). We met the remarkable Mr. Taylor earlier. Presumably this larger house was built to raise his growing family. One of his sons, Telford Taylor, was the chief prosecutor at the Nuremburg Trials after World War II. In choosing the architectural firm of Russell and Rice, Taylor enriched the heritage of Schenectady by bequeathing us a design from the board of one of the major archi-

FIG. 191   *The Albert Levi house (1910).*

FIG. 192 Interior of the Levi house.

ALBERT J. LEVI

FIG. 193 Albert Levi in Schenectady Just For Fun.

tects of the early twentieth century. Ambrose J. Russell was born in the East Indies to missionary parents in 1857 but raised and educated in Glasgow. His architectural training was at the *Ecole des Beaux Arts*, and upon his migration to the United States in 1884, he worked for one year in the studio of Henry Hobson Richardson. For a short time he was active in Worcester, Massachusetts, but he soon moved, first to Kansas City and finally to the Pacific Northwest. In conjunction with a succession of junior partners, he was responsible for many major buildings and residences on the Seattle and Tacoma skylines (fig. 195). The Taylor house exudes the quiet symmetry of the Colonial Imitation style, but the central gable in the roof, with its large, round arch, is something we have not seen before. Compare this with a similar central gable on the Sargent House (fig. 99). There the gable is steep in the Victorian tradition; here we see a flatter gable, truer to the Georgian style. Elsewhere, a wide, three-part window over the doorway comes from the Greek Revival tradition, as does the entrance. The fanciful placement of a large, semicircular window in the gable is typical of the Colonial Revival. Holding to the Colonial Revival tradition, this house mixes motifs from various periods, but with so little ostentation that the effect is Colonial Imitation.

The Junggren house (1911), 1179 Lowell Road, presents another fascinating variation on the Colonial Imitation theme (fig. 196). In its three-bay plan with closely aligned dormers, the house resembles one group we have seen. Other details, however, contrast this façade with a Federal style Colonial Imitation. The modillions under the eaves and the offset brickwork at the corners in a "quoined" effect are drawn from the Georgian period (fig. 197). Most striking are the porch and entrance. The porch is much too large for the house—at least for a Federal style house—and reminds one of the overblown circular porch on the Vedder house (fig. 112). The door is a beautiful example of design motifs which originated in the English Arts and Crafts movement and which we will see employed in the Bungalow style (fig. 198).

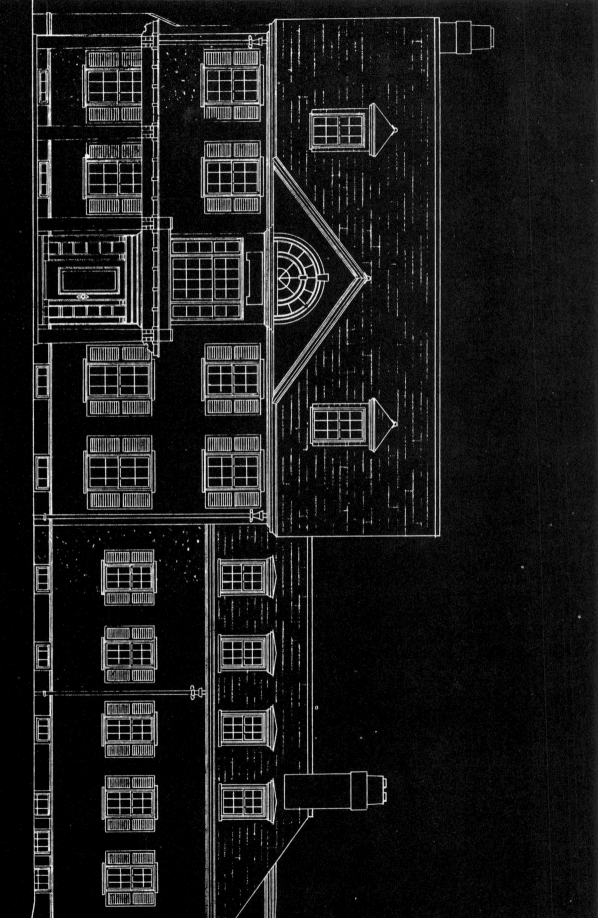

EAST.

The successful generation of large amounts of power was crucial in the practical application of electricity and the expansion of the electrical industry. Oscar Junggren, when he died in 1935, was credited with the almost single-handed development of the large turbines which generated nine-tenths of the nation's electric power. Born in Sweden in 1865, he came to work in 1889 for the Edison Electric Company in New York. In 1891, he was engaged by the General Electric Company as an engineer and draftsman. In 1902-1903, he was a chief designing engineer. He collaborated with W.L.R. Emmet in the construction of the then huge Curtis Turbine. Many said this titan could not be built: its generation capacity of 5000 kilowatts exceeded all predecessors by ten-fold. When completed and installed in Chicago, it was hailed as "the greatest single step forward in power plant progress since James Watt invented the steam engine." Such was the importance of Junggren's achievement that, during its trials, "General Electric stock rose when it ran and fell when it did not." From 1924 to 1932, thirty new turbines, each separately designed and more powerful than the last, were designed by Junggren—an average of one every four months. A holder of 130 patents, he was a mechanical genious of the first rank. (fig. 199).

In this chapter we have examined a distinct style representing the logical culmination of a residential architecture which complemented an intense spirit of nationalism that had developed in the last quarter of the nineteenth century and extended well into the twentieth. We have seen a smooth evolution from the Queen Anne, through the Colonial Revival, into the Colonial Imitation. In later chapters we will examine houses exemplifying alternate design systems that, while rejecting the Colonial Imitation style, sought the essence of the truly "American" home.

FIG. 194 Preliminary sketch of the Taylor house (1911) by Russell and Rice. This drawing, not a working drawing, was intended to allow Taylor to visualize the design.

FIG. 195 Early photograph of the Governor's Mansion, Olympia, Washington, by Russell and Babcock (1909). Russell's facility with the Colonial Revival style is evident.

FIG. 198   The entrance of the Junggren house was inspired by the English Arts and Crafts movement.

FIG. 199   Oscar Junggren (1865-1935).

FIG. 197   Junggren house, detail.

FIG. 196   The Oscar Junggren house (1911).

CHAPTER VII

The Gambrel Roof

A gambrel roof has two slopes on each side, a short upper slope of low pitch and a long lower slope of steep pitch. The name may have come from the resemblance of the angle thus formed to the gambrel, or hock of a horse's hind leg, though it more possibly derives from the old French 'gamberel,' a crooked stick used by butchers.

Hugh Morrison

FIG. 200 *The Rickey-Whitestone house (c. 1902), 7 Douglas Road. This photograph was taken shortly after the house was completed.*

The original purpose of the gambrel roof was economy. The flatter upper section required less lumber than if the steeper section were extended to a peak. From the earliest days New England homes commonly used this roof, with the upper and lower section being of about equal length, while the Dutch gambrel used a shorter upper section.[1] The gambrel roof died out by the Federal period, but it was revived in the Queen Anne period. The Queen Anne gambrel descends over the house, enveloping and unifying the design: it conveys the feeling that the house is hugging the ground. Today, the gambrel roof has become firmly linked with the Dutch Colonial tradition. All gambrel roofed houses are "Dutch Colonial" in real estate parlance, especially in an area originally settled by the Dutch. Architects in the Queen Anne period, however, were not consciously imitating a Colonial gambrel. Only in later periods, when Queen Anne was superseded by Colonial Revival and Colonial Imitation, did gambrel roofs become synonymous with Dutch architecture. In this chapter we will watch this evolution in the Realty Plot.

The gambrel roofs of the Rickey-Whitestone (c. 1902) and Stewart houses (1906) come all the way down to the first story (figs. 200-204). The second story is completely incorporated within the roof; this unifying of the first and second story is a design tenet of the Queen Anne style. The Rickey-Whitestone house has as a Colonial influence only a Georgian style balustrade on the original porch. The rest of the house, including the bay windows and second story skirting over the

first is Queen Anne. The large wrap-around porch on the Stewart house is Queen Anne. Both employ a cruciform roof of four intersecting gables which has no Colonial (certainly no Dutch Colonial) precedent, and both have acquired some measure of overall symmetry from the Colonial Revival.

Abraham Gifford's house (1905), 1386 Lowell Road, like these two houses, is quite symmetrical above the first floor with its two dormers (fig. 205). In contrast, the ground floor has asymmetrically placed openings. So striking is this disparity that one wonders whether, somehow, two different designs have been grafted together. The "Dutch door" suggests that there was some intention to view this house as Dutch, but these doors were common from the 1800's onward in any style. Finally, the dormers are not the shed dormers associated with Dutch houses. Like the preceding two examples, this house fits squarely in the Queen Anne.

The Herbert Walker house (c. 1902), 1124 Avon Road, once again shows a dramatic descending gambrel roof that acts as an umbrella over the design (figs. 206, 207). Shingles, a wrap-around porch, Queen Anne style windows, an oriel window on the west elevation, and a prominent, molded chimney are all Queen Anne characteristics. The Warren Conover house (1905), 1234 Lowell Road, is also prominently asymmetrical and, therefore, Queen Anne (fig. 208). The only Colonial features are the Greek Revival style entrance which might be the result of later remodeling. Note the interesting dormer on the right. If its roof were a continuation of the upper slope of the main roof, it would be a Dutch style dormer;

155

FIG. 201 Alterations performed by the Whitestones in 1916 added the present oriel window on the second floor and the porte-cochere. The wooden balustrades have been lost.

FIG. 202 Interior of the Rickey-Whitestone house showing the Rickeys' furnishings purchased specifically for this house. Walter Rickey lived here for only one year before leaving the area. Samuel Whitestone was Comptroller of the General Electric Company.

*FIG. 203   The Samuel Stewart house (1906),
1183 Stratford Road. This and the following
photograph were taken around 1910.*

FIG. 204   *View of the hall, Stewart house.*

FIG. 205 *The Gifford house (1905).*

159

FIG. 206   The Herbert Walker house (c. 1902) is a transitional design between the Queen Anne and the Colonial Revival. Its Colonial Revival features include a Palladian window symmetrically placed above two bay windows in the street gable.

FIG. 207   Herbert Walker house. The exquisite oriel window is visible on the right.

FIG. 208   The Warren Conover house (1905). The house has been aluminum sided.

but its width approaches the continuous dormer of the Bungalow style. The architect, Cortland Van Rensselaer, is responsible for several homes with prominent Bungalow features.

Frank H. Gale was the Advertising Manager of General Electric before his retirement in 1933. Gale originally worked as a draftsman until he was transferred to the Commercial Department in 1899. In 1901 he was placed in charge of the company's interests at the Pan-American Exposition in Buffalo. Subsequently, he managed all such exhibitions and conventions for the company, notably the World's Fairs in St. Louis and San Francisco. His exhibit in San Francisco earned him a gold medal. Drawing on his experience as a draftsman, Gale served as architect for his house. The design is conservative (fig. 209). A greater symmetry shows the influence of the Colonial Revival but otherwise the house clings to the Queen Anne with its shingle siding, wide windows, (multipaned above), and skirting of the second story over the first. Given the absence of any Colonial motifs, it is difficult to believe Gale was recalling a Dutch Colonial heritage in his choice of roof.

These houses have a gambrel roof which makes no apparent reference to a Colonial style; it would be inaccurate to call them "Dutch Colonial"—they

FIG. 209   The Frank H. Gale house (1906), 1168 Lowell Road.

FIG. 210   The Jesse Patton house (1903), 1120 Adams Road. On the interior, the paneled dining room is circular and, as a lavish extra, the flooring is curved to follow the shape of the room. Such craftsmanship for its own sake (custom-curved flooring adds nothing structurally) was typical in this period. These houses should be viewed as enormous pieces of antique furniture.

FIG. 211 Entrance of the Patton house.

are Queen Anne buildings. As the Colonial Revival style emerged, we find a group of houses whose roofs are transitional between the older Queen Anne gambrel and the emerging Dutch Colonial Imitation gambrel. The architects of these houses may have been conscious of the ancestry of the gambrel roof, but they made no attempt to duplicate a Dutch Colonial style accurately. In the case of the Patton house (1903), for instance, the gambrel has been reduced to a single dormer (figs. 210, 211). Jesse Patton was a partner in the firm of Patton and Hall, a bootery on State Street that was one of the largest shoe dealerships in our area of the state (fig. 212). In later years he was familiar to his neighbors as a nervous man who frequently backed his large car out of his driveway into the tree across the street. This house is an excellent example of the Colonial Revival style: hipped roof and colossal pilasters are drawn from the Georgian period; a Federal style fanlight sits over a Victorian style double-leafed door; and Federal style, paired colonnettes are set on a broad Victorian porch. The gambrel dormer is purely decorative, and it is possible that its inclusion here is related to its use in the William Pearson house (1902), 1125 Wendell Avenue, which was built two years earlier (fig. 213). The architect of the Pearson house, however, had used a gambrel for the entire roof, so that its use in a dormer there was at least consistent.

The Pearson house roof makes no attempt to engulf the second floor; it seems apparent that this is a thoroughly Colonial Revival design in which a Victorian architect, seeking originality, has included an "Old Colonial" gambrel. If this is supposed to be a Colonial gambrel, its New England configuration, with an equal upper and lower slope, may either have been intentional or because architect and client were not aware of

FIG. 212 Advertisement for Patton and Hall.

FIG. 214   William Pearson house, detail. A Dutch gambrel is selected for the dormer while an English gambrel is employed in the main roof. This suggests that the selection of the Dutch gambrel was deliberate.

FIG. 213   The William Pearson house (1902), 1125 Wendell Avenue.

the regional variations in the design. This latter explanation is possible, for much of the scholarly research and restoration of Colonial architecture has occurred more recently. True to the style, there is an asymmetry in the placement of windows which is not at first apparent. Note how Federal and Georgian motifs are juxtaposed where delicate Adam style garlands surmount a Palladian window (fig. 214).

The Potter-Coolidge house (1904), another transitional Colonial Revival design, utilizes a broken segmental arch in the porch—a Georgian motif taken, in turn, from seventeenth-century Italian architecture where such a porch might shelter the

entrance to a Baroque church (fig. 215). The doorway itself is Greek Revival. The lower edge of the roof is continuous with the standard Queen Anne skirting of the second floor over the first and may refer to the flaring of a true Dutch Colonial roof.

William Coolidge (see Chapter IX) purchased this house in 1928. To it, he welcomed a steam of callers who came from all over the world to visit the Research Laboratory. In 1929, Madame Curie visited Schenectady. She had become ill in Detroit, her previous stop. It was feared that another public reception like the one she received there, where an admirer had torn off a piece of her coat and her laundry had vanished after she had sent it out, would further weaken her. Thus, she was spirited off the train in Amsterdam and driven by Dr. Coolidge to his Lenox Road home, where she recuperated for three days in secrecy. Coolidge wrote,

"Arrived at our home, I ran to the door and called out to Dorothy [Mrs. Coolidge] that Madame Curie was here. Dorothy was so sure that I was joking, that I had difficulty in convincing here that I wasn't. . . . There were complications, as our guest facilities are limited, and my parents were visiting us at the time . . . but Madame Curie was immediately put to bed in our room."

The first owner was William Bancroft Potter, for thirty-five years Engineer of the Railway Department of General Electric (fig. 216). In that post, he handled the engineering involved in such large projects as the electrification of Grand Central Terminal in New York City. At the beginning of his career, the "horseless car" on street railway tracks was an astonishing oddity. Potter saw it become part of the American fabric. "His contributions to the electric traction art were basic, and hence enduring."

FIG. 215 *The Potter-Coolidge house (1904,*

1480 Lenox Road.

In the Walter Moody house (1903), 1033 Avon Road, symmetry, violated in the street façade only by a bay window tucked under the porch on the left, is the fingerprint of Colonial Revival influence (fig. 217). No specific colonial motifs can be identified. The three dormers with truncated roofs are a standard Richardsonian design; they interrupt a three-sloped roof. This design once again creates the illusion that the roof is pressing the building down into the ground.

The second owner was Francis J. Cole, Chief Mechanical Engineer of the American Locomotive Company. Cole improved the design of the superheated steam locomotive. Steam passed through special tubes that raised its heat so that, when it was in the engine cyclinder, less condensa-

FIG. 216 *William Bancroft Potter (1863-1934).*

FIG. 217 *The Moody house (1903). The protruding, symmetrical dormers create a powerful feeling and show the work of a mature architect who could draw the best from the Queen Anne and Colonial Revival traditions to create a totally new effect.*

FIG. 218 *The 50,000th engine produced by the American Locomotive Company was designed by Francis Cole and completed in 1910.*

tion occurred near the end of the piston cycle. This yielded higher efficiency. Cole was one of the nation's foremost locomotive designers. In the same year he moved onto Avon Road, he created ALCO's 50,000th engine, the first ever to use cast-steel cylinders (fig. 218). What lively debates the neighbors Cole and Moody must have had over the future of steam and electricity in rail transport!

In the next group, the houses follow a Dutch Colonial pattern. Most obvious in this regard is the home of Edwin A. Baldwin, one-time vice-President in charge of the European Department of International General Electric (fig. 219). This house is a Colonial Imitation style dwelling that makes clear reference to a Dutch Colonial building tradition. Besides a Dutch gambrel roof, the house also has simple gables that are typical of a Dutch farm house and wide shingles, possibly taken from a Dutch source (fig. 220). For whatever reason, the Dutch Colonial design was not carried through the doorway, which is a correct Georgian copy. The house is built with the narrow side toward the street to take advantage of the shape of the lot. True, in some places, such as early Charleston, property taxes were based on front footage, but such was not the case in Schenectady. The architect made no historical allusion when he oriented the house in this fashion.

Dutch builders frequently tied a shed dormer to the upper slope of a gambrel roof. Because the architect has used such dormers, there is no question he was thinking of Dutch sources in designing the William Ely house (c. 1901), 1049 Avon Road (figs. 221, 222). This house is an early example of the Dutch Colonial Imitation style that was popular after 1920. At some later time, significant modifications to the entrance were made which

FIG. 219 *The Edwin Baldwin house (1912), 1374 Lowell Road.*

FIG. 220   Truncated gables, in which the peak
of the gable has been cut off, are characteristic
of Dutch architecture.

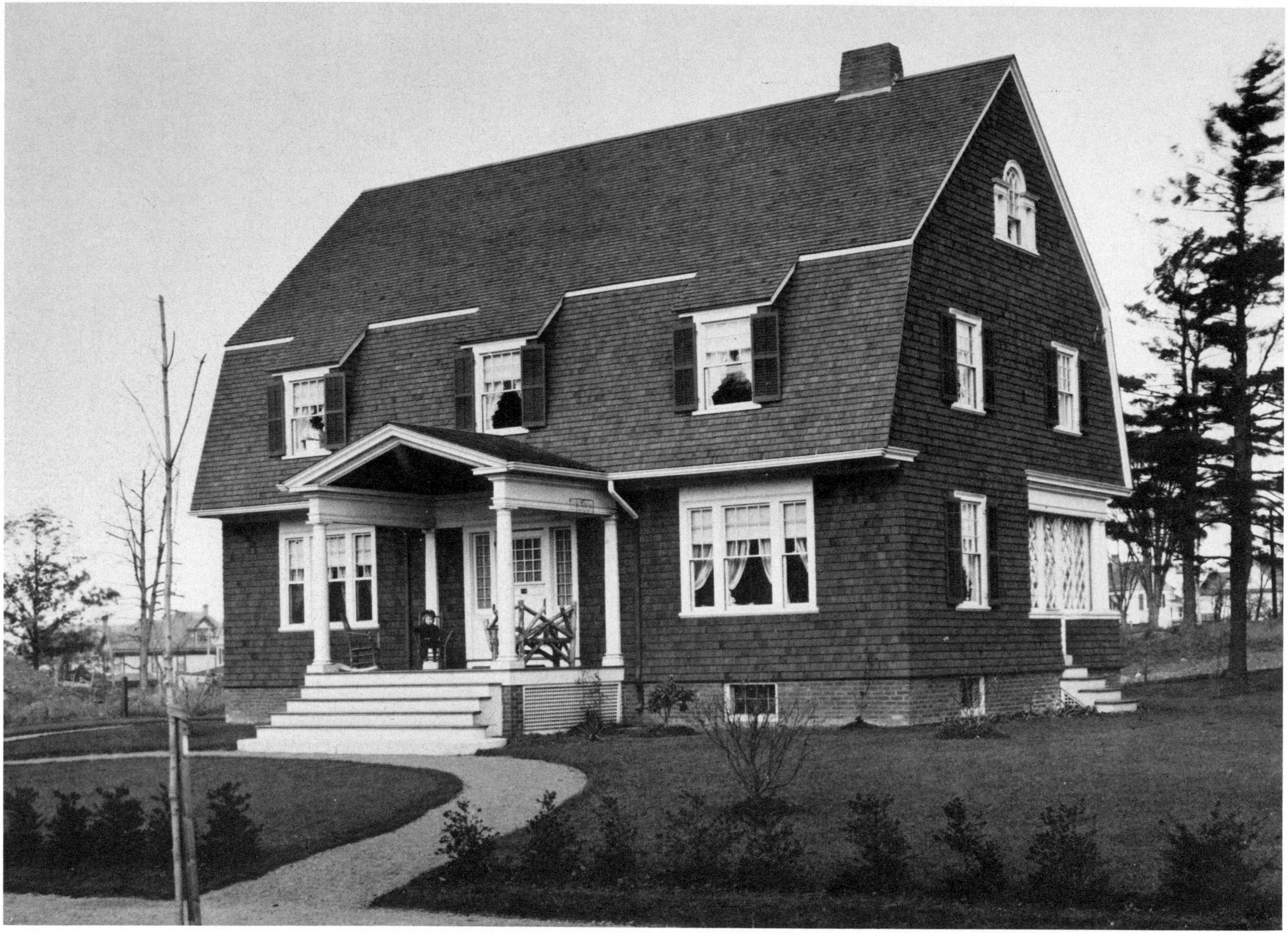

FIG. 222   *Interior of the Ely house in 1904.*

FIG. 221   *The Ely house is a remarkable design for the year 1901. The early date might be inferred, however, from the rather oversized porch and the depressed Palladian window, a signature of the Colonial Revival style, which can be seen in the gable end. Photograph taken in 1904.*

171

FIG. 223 *Present appearance of the Ely house. This is a clear example of the contrast between the heavier, deeper porch of the Colonial Revival style and the more delicate entrance treatment of the Colonial Imitation style.*

FIG. 224 *Dr. E. MacDonald Stanton.*

augment the Colonial Imitation styling. Of interest, the renovated porch is Federal with a molded wooden fan in place of a fanlight window, in keeping with the preference for Federal detailing in the Realty Plot (fig. 223).

The second owner of this house was Dr. E. MacDonald Stanton, a practicing surgeon for over fifty years. In addition to his professional duties, he was a civic leader, serving both on the board and as President of the Chamber of Commerce. He was Chairman of the Schenectady Planning Commission, and he arbitrated labor issues at the American Locomotive Company. In 1947 he received a merit award from Iowa State College, his alma mater, for his role in settling a strike at General Electric (fig. 224).

J. WEBER.
ELECTRIC FIXTURE
Filed July 26, 1927.

Fig. 1. Fig. 2. Fig. 3. Fig. 4. Fig. 5.

Inventor
John Weber.

FIG. 227   Patent drawing.

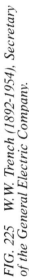

FIG. 225   W.W. Trench (1892-1954), Secretary of the General Electric Company.

The third occupant, William W. Trench, in addition to serving as Secretary of the General Electric Company for twenty-four years, fathered many innovations, among which was the suggestions system. Like Dr. Stanton, he was a civic leader. Mayor Wemple said at his death, "He was a tireless worker in behalf of the welfare of his community, his state, and his nation. His distinguished service as Chairman of the City Planning Commission and as chairman of local war bonds drives will always be remembered. Many of his contributions to local civic improvements will have an everlasting effect upon our city's progress. His kindly, genial spirit and his concern for his fellow man endeared him to all who knew him" (fig. 225).

The John Weber house (1906), 1204 Rugby Road, has shed dormers in a Dutch colonial roof similar to the Ely house (fig. 226). The windows are done in the Queen Anne fashion, multipaned above, single below. Notice how the use of square panes in the upper sash is sustained throughout while the exact number of panes and their size vary. John Weber ran the Weber Electric Company in partnership with his brother, August (fig. 55). Although primarily involved in administration, he is credited with several patents for designs of light sockets (fig. 227).

An interesting story is attached to figure 228, a newspaper photograph of John Weber. He is holding the whistle that summoned workers to the Edison shops at 7:00 A.M. and relieved them at 6:00 P.M. Additionally, its range made it the "official time piece" for city residents. When Superintendent W.B. "Pop" Turner left Edison's employ to start an iron foundry, he took the whistle. His venture failed, however, and in 1895 the Weber family bought his building for their porcelain works. The whistle was boxed and stored, and later presented to Henry Ford when the auto magnate visited Schenectady in 1935. Accompanied by Steinmetz's adopted grandson, Joseph Hayden, Dr. Coolidge, Dr. Everett Lee, and Roy C. Muir, Ford visited the Realty Plot home of Charles P. Steinmetz. Subsequently, he was pleased to include the whistle among his other memorabilia of

Edison at his museum in Dearborn, Michigan, and he came to August Weber's house to collect the artifact. "That was an exciting day for everyone," recalls August Weber's stepdaughter, Lucy Reynolds Carichoff. The photograph was taken in 1949 at a dinner honoring the nine remaining Edison Pioneers in Schenectady. These men, including John Weber, had worked with Edison before 1892 in Schenectady or Menlo Park.

The Webers were not the only brothers to live in the Realty Plot: John and James Parker lived in houses at 1188 and 1178 Lowell Road. Their father, John Nicholaus Parker, had been the Superintendent of the Barge Canal and owner of the Craig

FIG. 226   The John Weber house (1906).

175

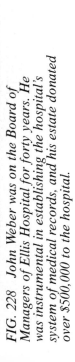

FIG. 229 *The Parker Building (1906), now the Phillips Building, is still Schenectady's tallest.*

FIG. 228 *John Weber was on the Board of Managers of Ellis Hospital for forty years. He was instrumental in establishing the hospital's system of medical records, and his estate donated over $500,000 to the hospital.*

177

Hotel which stood near the Rexford bridge. The family built and owned the Parker building in downtown Schenectady (fig. 229). James Parker's house has a Dutch gambrel roof; the rest of the house combines Queen Anne and Colonial Revival features in a familiar manner (fig. 230). The house was constructed while the Parkers were on an extended honeymoon tour of Europe. Both brothers were involved in politics. John was District Attorney from 1917 to 1922 (fig. 231); James, who died in an automobile accident in 1941, was prominent in real estate and insurance as well as politics. (He served as Treasurer of the Schenectady County Republican Party.)

As the Colonial Revival underwent a transition to the Colonial Imitation, the Queen Anne gambrel, now viewed as a Dutch Colonial gambrel, became more formalized and symmetrical. The Edward F. Peck house (1909), 1333 Lowell Road, and the Albert Vedder house (1912) 1296 Lowell Road, have both lost all the asymmetry of the Victorian picturesque (figs. 232, 233). Yet, in a more apparent way than in the other Colonial Imitation designs, this style imitates no specific period of the past. The central gable, never quite the same on any two, may have a gambrel roof as in the Vedder house, a triangular pediment as in the Peck house, or some variation of a large dormer as in the James Parker house. Whatever its form, there is no historical precedent for this large central feature grafted to a Dutch colonial dwelling. These houses, with such idiosyncrasies as the architecturally inappropriate but socially necessary side porch on the Vedder house, can only be understood in terms of the singular period in which they were built.

JOHN R. PARKER

FIG. 231 John Parker from Schenectady Just For Fun. He lived nearby at 1188 Lowell Road.

FIG. 230 The James Parker house (1908), 1178 Lowell Road, has symmetrical Dutch shed dormers, a wrap-around porch of Richardsonian masonry, asymmetrically disposed polygonal bays, and a Federal fanlight over the entrance. This is a photograph taken by the architect when the house was completed to "advertise his wares" to prospective clients.

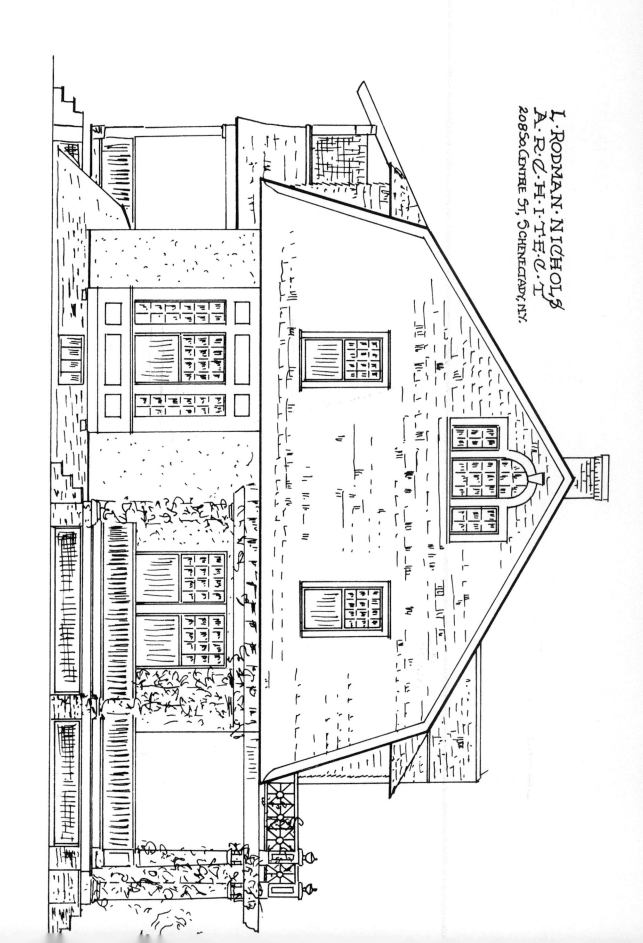

LEFT·ELEVATION

L·RODMAN·NICHOLS
A·R·C·H·I·T·E·C·T
208 So. Centre St, Schenectady, N.Y.

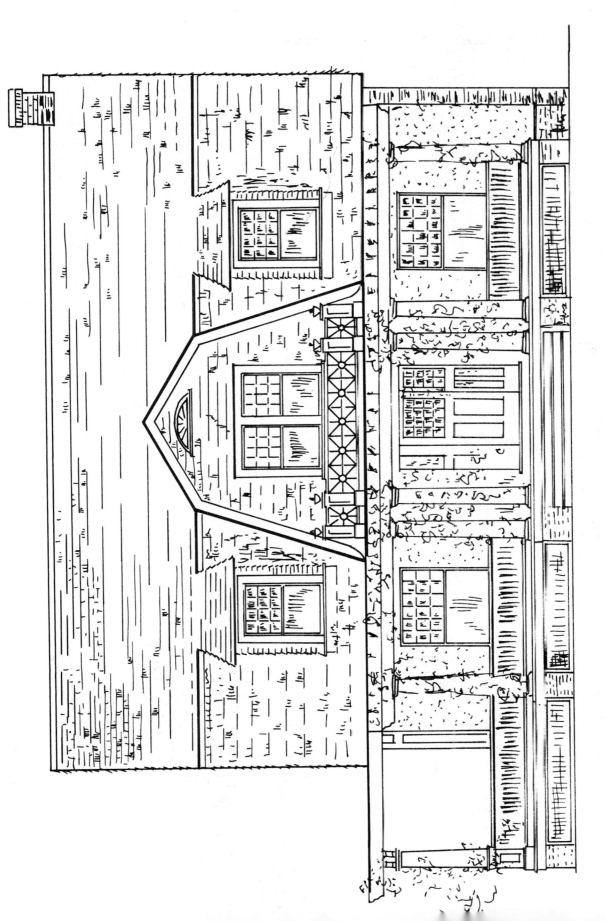

FRONT·ELEVATION

FIG. 233 *The Albert Vedder house (1912) in a*
preliminary drawing.

Elmwood & Peck

E. F. PECK

FIG. 234 Edward Folger Peck from Schenectady Just For Fun.

Edward Folger Peck was for ten years the General Manager of the Schenectady Railway Company. He was hired by the company for his organizational talents, evinced in his rehabilitation of the Kings County Electric Light and Power Company in Brooklyn. He was an assertive executive, and after he left the Schenectady Railway Company, he opened an independent consulting firm to revitalize ailing utilities. George Emmons, General Manager of the Edison Works, had said the city needed an expanded, inexpensive trolley to accommodate his workers if General Electric was to prosper. Peck's task was to extend the system: this he did with a network of interurban and suburban trains, as well as with lines to every neighborhood (fig. 234). Sometimes there was opposition from those who said children "would be ground and mangled under the merciless wheels," but Peck was able to use his persuasive personality to carry the day for the railway company. When, in 1903, citizens of Scotia complained about poor lighting on Mohawk Avenue, he quickly agreed with them and installed electric street lights within one month at no charge to the town. Such acts would be remembered when it came time to lay new track.

The trolley system was an essential public service at the turn of the century; and, by 1921, electric railways were the fifth largest industry in the nation. George Lunn's rise to mayor was due in part to his opposition to a fare increase of one penny. It was the only transportation to work, and it liberated the entire family to shop downtown or to visit area parks. The coming of the automobile caused a rapid demise of the trolley. It is difficult today to gauge Edward Peck's importance to the community now that public transportation has become a subsidized, unsavory alternative for an energy-conscious public.

Another resident of the Realty Plot whose legacy is still with us was Tullock Townsend, a civil engineer who was Assistant Superintendent of

FIG. 232 The Edward Peck house (1909), early photograph.

FIG. 235 *Tullock Townsend (1888-1966).*

Schools for twenty-nine years (fig. 235). In this position he sat on the school board as business manager with responsibility for the construction and maintenance of schools. Townsend worked with Charles Steinmetz, another school board member, in realizing some of Steinmetz's forward-looking dreams (such as the one-story school with safety exits to the outside in each room). Townsend agreed that children needed fresh air and exercise off dangerous city streets. For this reason, land was purchased around the schools, and in Schenectady there is a playground adjacent to each school.

We have seen how some of the most interesting houses here were built by people with associations to the construction industry. This house is no exception. It has a three-bay, gambrel design with complete Colonial Imitation symmetry and a carefully copied Federal doorway. Beyond this, it is an ingeniously worked-out design (fig. 236). The eye is carried from the bay windows on the first floor, through the diagonal lines of the porch roof, and upward to a semicircular dormer window of the type made popular by Richardson in the Queen Anne period. The house is plaster covered, but there is none of the amorphous quality of some plaster dwellings. It is a compact and handsome design.

Townsend spent $34,000 to build it in 1923—by his own admission, too much to have paid. Initially it had a coal furnace in the house and another one in the garage to keep his car warm enough to start in the winter. Later, the furnace in the house was replaced with two oil burners—Townsend wanted an extra in case the other would not work. While the house was being built, Mrs. Gilbert, from down the block, came to practice her Italian with the cabinetmaker who was handcarving the moldings. As he was paying him twenty dollars per day, Townsend was infuriated that she was wasting the worker's time, but he kept still to remain on good terms with his new neighbors. Steinmetz stopped by daily in the year of his death to watch the progress on his friend's home; H.W. Darling, always watchdog for the Schenectady Realty Company, offered to lend money to Townsend so he could build a bigger house, but the offer was politely declined.

A vernacular style, similar to that of this house, combining a Dutch gambrel roof with a continuous, Bungalow style dormer was quite popular until the Second World War. In the inflationary period that followed, the gambrel roof disappeared because it was more costly than a single-pitched roof.

FIG. 236 The Townsend house (1923), 1089 Avon Road.

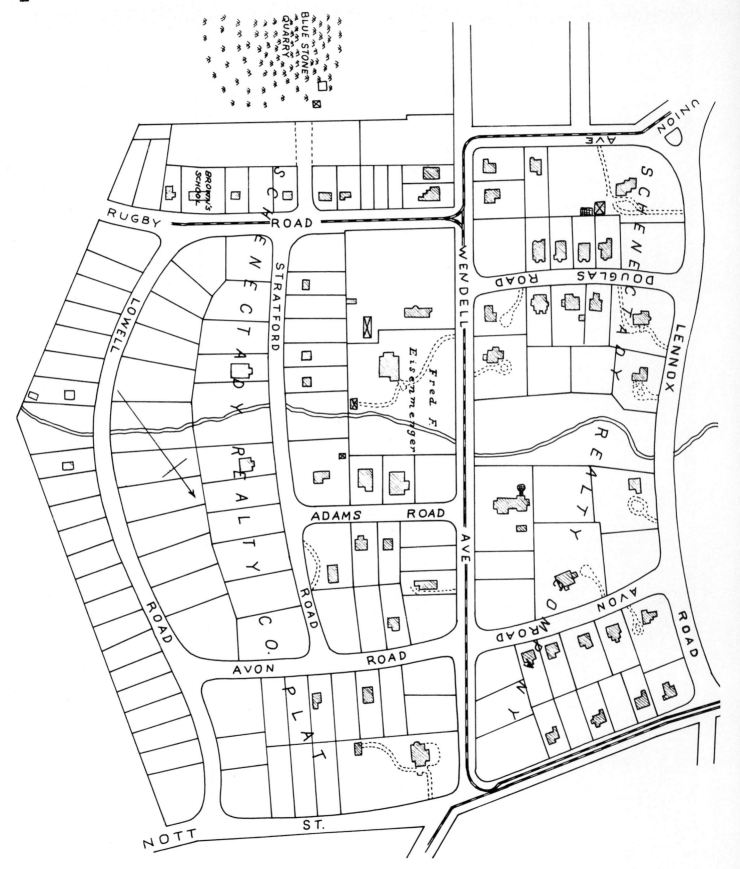

CHAPTER VIII

The House Without a Kitchen Chimney

The most important house in the Realty Plot is the second house built for H.W. Hillman in 1905, for this house was built as an experiment by Mr. Hillman to prove his thesis that electricity could have wide domestic applications beyond providing illumination. Paradoxically, the house was not built in the more prevalent colonial style of its neighbors, but was constructed in the Bungalow style. Before turning to the Hillman house, let us look at the Bungalow style and the houses built according to its principles in the Realty Plot.

The Bungalow style, as we shall define it, was a composite of several similar architectural movements. Principal among them were: the English Arts and Crafts movement headed by William Morris, the American Arts and Crafts movement championed by Gustav Stickley in his influential magazine *The Craftsman*, and the California Bungalow-Mission style of Greene and Greene. Because these sects worked on friendly terms and borrowed freely from each other, their minor distinctions need not concern us. Practitioners of the style adhered to several basic tenets which make this an easy style to identify. They rejected the elaborate ornamentation of the Victorian and Colonial Revival period and clung to simple, straight lines and "honest" construction in which structural elements were exposed for all to see. A Bungalow house has massive exposed beams in the living room and roof rafters and brackets that can be seen in the eaves (fig. 238). There was an emphasis of the horizontal to tie the house to the earth. Frank Lloyd Wright's Prairie style falls loosely into the Bungalow category. Explaining this emphasis on the horizontal, he stated: "We of the Middle West are living on the prairie . . . and we shall recognize and accentuate this natural beauty, its quiet level. Hence, gently sloping roofs, low proportions. . . ." Bungalows are usually one-story affairs. "Natural" materials such as field stone or shingles were used, and these elements of the Queen Anne—the Bungalow style has been typified as the final evolutionary phase of the Queen Anne—were blended with a Modern desire for functionalism and symmetry.

Although influences of the style have been noted in numerous other houses, only eight homes are close enough to the "genuine article" to merit inclusion here. This paucity does not reflect the true popularity of a style which began around 1900 and swept the country in the first quarter of this century, but it does emphasize the point that Bungalows were intended to be modest, inexpensive dwellings. Someone planning a substantial city residence would not usually contemplate a style that glorified humble virtues. There are few truly typical Bungalows in the Realty Plot, and were it not for the questing, iconoclastic intellects who built here, there would undoubtedly be fewer examples still.

The R.E. Russell house (1908), 1280 Stratford Road, is a Bungalow through and through (fig. 239). The roof descending toward the street, the

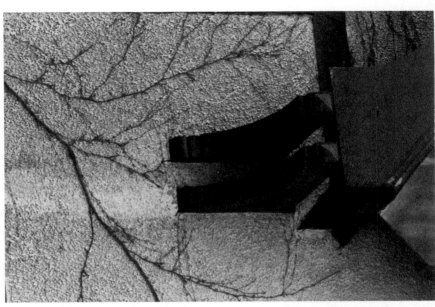

FIG. 238   *Brackets in the eaves of the Haskins house (1914), 1188 Avon Road.*

FIG. 239   *The R.E. Russell house (1908).*

FIG. 240   Interior of the Russell house.

continuous porch across the front, the use of shingles, the simple, wooden, porch columns, and the continuous dormer in the second story give this house all of the elements of a typical Bungalow. Only wide eaves with supporting brackets are missing, and we must presume that Russell had personal reasons for omitting them. The reason for the unpopularity of this style in the Realty Plot is apparent. The house is far less dramatic than its immediate neighbors, and this raises the question why the house was built as it was.

The answer probably lies with the background of Russell. Although at the time of his death in 1922 he was manager of Tungar sales, he was not an upper-echelon employee of General Electric when he built the house. His father, Sol Smith Russell, was a prominent actor of the 1890's, and money from this source was used to purchase the land and build the dwelling. R.E. Russell had a keen interest in architecture. He had worked as a draftsman before coming to Schenectady, and with this background, he drew plans which suited the limited budget and avant-garde taste of a man from an artistic background. The inside of the house has a wonderfully open quality with window seats, beamed ceilings, and wainscoting taken entirely from the Arts and Crafts movement (figs. 240, 241). The marvelous warmth and interest of rooms done in this style are again attracting the attention they deserve.

Albert Burtiss's house (1904), 1169 Stratford Road, could have been included with the section on Modern architecture, but is placed here as it demonstrates how the Bungalow style could be altered to suit fashionable tastes in the Realty Plot (figs. 242, 243). Albert Burtiss, owner of the "Burtiss Block" which stands at 148-152 Jay Street, operated a hardware store there. After his death in 1914, his son Benjamin lived on Stratford Road. The younger Burtiss sold Huppmobiles at one of the first automobile dealerships in Schenectady; in 1919, according to the July 4th *Gazette*, he died in Los Angeles while on a "motor trip" undertaken to benefit his health (fig. 244).

188

FIG. 241 *Interior of the Russell house.*

This house has an unorthodox design. A swooping Bungalow roof terminates in a heavy-pillared porch; long, broad proportions also signal a Bungalow, and the band of dormer windows across the front could have been an early creation of Frank Lloyd Wright. Any Dutch inflection which might have been lent by a gambrel roof has been buried by the lavish materials of the building, which include expensive, cream-colored, Roman brick and a massive hinged door (fig. 245). Tucked on the south side is a small Queen Anne tower which is not allowed to interrupt the roof.

Elements of the Bungalow style did creep into the Realty Plot as isolated segments. For instance, the 1909 renovation of the Broderick house (fig. 102) uses high brick piers with massive wooden columns to support the front porch. The high pier was a standard feature of the Bungalow style; its use in the Broderick house is a subtle clue that the porch was altered. The Hooker house (fig. 59) has not only the high pier but also textured brick, another characteristic of the style. The Charles Fair house (1916), 1422 Lowell Road, is yet another hybrid due to remodeling (fig. 246). Charles Van Brunt, the second owner's son and an architect in Kansas City, directed renovation while convalescing from a fracture of the spine in 1928. This is a three-bay Colonial Imitation house, and the dormers are academically correct replicas of the modest dormers on a true Federal home, but the boldly projecting porch roof has no historical precedent. It is supported by large brackets in the Bungalow fashion, and similar brackets support an inorganic oriel window (figs. 247, 248). These brackets became an extremely popular way of supporting eaves throughout the country on houses of every style.

The Carichoff house (1914) is a five-bay Colonial Imitation home with a Dutch gambrel roof, but it also has prominent, insistent Bungalow overtones (fig. 249). The continuous shed dormer is a conspicuous feature of the Bungalow style; even more characteristic is the entrance composition. A bold gable over the porch supported by strong piers signals the style, and slender windows around

FIG. 242   The Albert Burtiss house (1904).

FIG. 243 Albert Burtiss house, detail.

B. A. BURTISS

FIG. 244 Benjamin Burtiss in Schenectady Just For Fun.

FIG. 246 The Charles Fair house (1916), 1422 Lowell Road. The entrance portico is not original. It was remodeled in the Bungalow style in 1928.

FIG. 245 Front door of the Burtiss house showing massive wrought iron hinges.

FIG. 247   Entrance of the Fair house.

the doorway were taken from the English Arts and Crafts (fig. 250). Carichoff built the Bradt house (fig. 171) and the Junggren house (fig. 196) on speculation, but the Avon Road home remained in the family until 1926. It may be significant that he commissioned more conservative works to ensure their sale while reserving this more experimental design for himself.

Although the Ferguson house (1914) qualifies as a three-bay Colonial Imitation design, the wide eaves, best seen in the dormers, and the chimney chopping up through these eaves are Bungalow in origin (figs. 251, 252). A Bungalow presents its broad, swooping roof toward the street, and there is a feeling of that roof here. Such long, low porches with massive columns became universal in the fully-evolved Bungalow style of the 1920's. The Fergusons were prominent in many areas. Charles Vaughn Ferguson was a scientist at the Research Laboratory for thirty-three years; Mrs. Ferguson was national President of the Girl Scouts of America from 1946 to 1952 (fig. 253); and C. Vaughn Ferguson, Jr., was a high-ranking State Department official and our ambassador to the Malagasy Republic.

The Frances Haskins residence (1914), 1188 Avon Road, shows further uses of ideas taken from the Bungalow style, but in many ways the architect has gone beyond reference to any particular style to create a totally original building (fig. 254).

FIG. 248 *Detail of the Fair house showing the oriel window added by Charles Van Brunt. Though the Bungalow style influenced his exterior changes, he chose Colonial Imitation designs inside and described his intentions in a letter to the interior decorator: "The [dining] room at present is trimmed in dark stained oak with a horrible dark red brick mantel and heavy, oak shelf. You know the type. The old oak trim is to be enameled. I am also tearing out the old brick on the mantel and installing a new wood mantel—colonial in design."*

FIG. 249 *The Eugene Carichoff house (1914), 1127 Avon Road.*

FIG. 250 *Porch and doorway of the Carichoff house. Compare this with figure 196.*

Half-timbering in the second story suggests the English Tudor style, while the asymmetry of the design and the polygonal bay suggest the Queen Anne style which was so closely allied with the Tudor Revival styles. Other elements are purely Bungalow. The porch composition is similar to the Carichoff house (fig. 249), and we have commented upon the brackets under the eaves. The one element that ties all of these design ideas together is the rectangular, regular arrangement of the half-timbers. This pattern not only is related to the Arts and Crafts movement, but shows a Modern attention to geometric forms after the Cubists. At a glance, any association of this house to Cubism seems far-fetched, but the longer one looks at the building, the more struck one becomes with those stark rectangles on its surface. That the architect, W.T.B. Mynderse, built several Colonial Imitation houses at about the same time shows his versatility as a designer (figs. 255-257).

The Haskins family has produced a number of talented scientists whose activities span a century of technological advances. As a young man, Caryl Davis Haskins worked in the shops of S.Z. de Ferranti, where he was involved with the first attempts to use alternating currents for electric lighting. After 1889 he was associated with Thomson-Houston Electric, and then General Electric, where he became head of the Instrument Department. His inventions in the area of metering electricity made an essential contribution. His father, John F. Haskins, was Ericsson's Chief Constructor on the *Monitor*, and he was one of the engineers in charge of boring the Hoosac Tunnel. The Haskins family lived on Washington Avenue in the present home of the Historical Society. In 1911, Caryl Haskins died suddenly.

FIG. 251 *The Ferguson house (1914), 1145 Avon Road.*

FIG. 253   *Mrs. Ferguson in girl scout garb.*

FIG. 252   *Ferguson house, detail.*

FIG. 254   The Frances Haskins house (1914).

FIG. 256 Mynderse's office on State Street was suitably cluttered in the Victorian fashion. the stuffed peacock, a symbol of Art Nouveau, was "Adam," a family pet until its death.

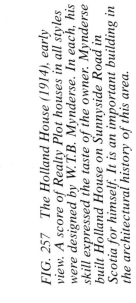

FIG. 255 William TenBroeck Mynderse (1871-1931). Mynderse was a linear descendant of Johannes Mynderse, a Dutch trader who came to Schenectady in 1700. He graduated from Union College in 1893 and completed his studies at the Metropolitan Architectural School, New York, three years later.

FIG. 257 The Holland House (1914), early view. A score of Realty Plot houses in all styles were designed by W.T.B. Mynderse. In each, his skill expressed the taste of the owner. Mynderse built Holland House on Sunnyside Road in Scotia for himself. It is an important building in the architectural history of this area.

FIG. 258   *The Andrew Averrett house (1909),*
1162 Rugby Road.

FIG. 259   *The Louis Wilson house (c. 1902),*
1065 Avon Road.

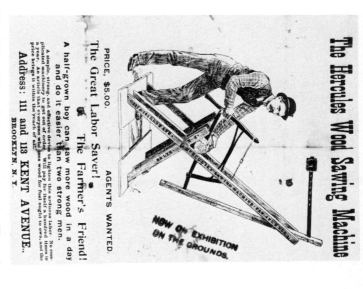

FIG. 260 Advertising poster for the Hercules Wood Sawing Machine.

His widow built the house on Avon Road three years later. Mrs. Haskins's son, Caryl Parker Haskins, studied the effects of radiation upon biological systems in the 1930's when this field was in its infancy. He established the Haskins Laboratory and headed the Carnegie Institution of Washington, D.C..

The Andrew Averrett house (1909), 1162 Rugby Road, is another hybrid design, wedding Bungalow style with Queen Anne style (fig. 258). On one side, the long roof of the Bungalow style slopes to cover a broad porch. The design has been interrupted on the left, however, with an asymmetrically-placed gable which surmounts a polygonal bay. Thus, the house has a truly split personality, one half drawn from the Queen Anne, the other from the Bungalow.

The earliest house in the Bungalow style is the Louis Wilson house (c. 1902) (fig. 259). The house is more closely allied with the English Arts and Crafts movement that preceded the true Bungalow style by a few years. Elements which would be used in the Bungalow style are seen here, including a prominent roof facing the street and brackets under the oriel windows. There is an intense interest in symmetry which removes the house from the Queen Anne style, and the house is almost devoid of any ornamentation. True to the Arts and Crafts movement, the design is created solely with structural elements such as the delicate mullions in the windows that vary from window to window to heighten interest.

Throughout this book, the careers of scientists who made major contributions to our present society through their association with the Research Laboratory of the General Electric Company have been highlighted. It is now appropriate to expand upon the significance of the Research Laboratory and its relation to the Realty Plot.

In 1750, beginning in Britain, a new system of industry emerged which centralized the means of production to increase productivity. It involved a radical improvement of the transportation network through the building of railroads and canals, and an expansion of power technology through the use of waterpower or coal-driven steam engines. This reorganization of society is called the Industrial Revolution. Side-by-side with the Industrial Revolution, a Scientific Revolution was occurring as men questioned traditional dogma and critically examined the physical world to unravel its mysteries. As new discoveries were made, their practical applications made an impact upon society either by introducing new products or improving old ones (fig. 260). This innovative process was termed "progress;" it was viewed as inevitable and beneficial. It was also haphazard, since nineteenth-century scientists and inventors worked independently and sporadically. A scientist might work until a single problem had been solved and might make no attempt to decipher a practical application of his discovery. An industrialist might use trial and error methods to improve a product, only to abandon his research when he succeeded in meeting his immediate need. There was no centralized, co-ordinated system of exploiting scientific discovery for commercial gain.

The formation of the Research Laboratory in 1900 in Schenectady inaugurated a second Industrial Revolution in this country. President Rice (fig. 29) told the stockholders in 1902: "It has been decided to establish a laboratory to do fundamental research in the belief that profitable discoveries will be made thereby." Edison originated the idea when he collected a group of bright men at his East Orange laboratory to tackle the technical problems of the application of electricity for illumination. By 1892, it was recognized that, in order to create an electric utility, a merger of the small, rival power companies was necessary. In that year the General Electric Company was formed from the Edison General Electric Company and the Thomson-Houston Company. In the following years it was realized that, unless "progress" was institutionalized by the company, new engineering developments might dwindle, causing the new industry based on innovative technology to flounder. To be sure, men of genius were already working for the enterprise, perfecting and expanding it. The incandescent lamp was produced in

His Only Rival.

General ⊕ Electric
MAZDA LAMP

FIG. 261   Mazda Lamp logo.

1879; the first central station to distribute electricity was put in operation in 1882; and the first commercial alternating current system was installed in 1887. But Edison's workshop had gathered tinkerers—it dealt only with applied science, not research. A true Research Laboratory would need to draw scientists from academe; philosophers of science would need to be enticed from their professorial robes into the market place.

Thirty-five years later, during the Great Depression, Thomas Linville, son-in-law of Edward Priest, and now living in the Wendell Avenue home (fig. 65), was Chief Engineer in charge of motor design. Submarines were powered by electric motors, and when the boat submerged, the electric power was supplied by a battery which had been charged while the boat was on the surface. Because business was slack, General Electric decided to enter this field, and Linville carried to Washington the Company's bid for a contract to build submarine motors. There he learned that his was not the low offer, but Linville was not deterred. A complicated bidding formula had been established by the government which awarded a premium to the motor that could run the longest underwater. He contacted his superior, William O. Shreve, who then owned the Carichoff house (fig. 249), and explained the situation. Linville believed that a more efficient design was possible; Shreve gave him the authority; and Linville changed the bid by guaranteeing greater performance. General Electric won the contract—which resulted in a loss of $485,000 as the company expended six months in arriving at a design to meet the specification. The long-term effect, however, was that General Electric built 98 percent of the submarine motors used by our navy in World War II. Linville became the nation's Chief Engineer for submarine motors, and he spent several months in the Pacific supervising repairs to the damage inflicted at Pearl Harbor.

By this time the importance of basic research to industry was clearly recognized, but in 1900 the concept was untried. Four men at General Electric advocated the establishment of the Research Laboratory: Elihu Thomson, of Lynn, Massachu-

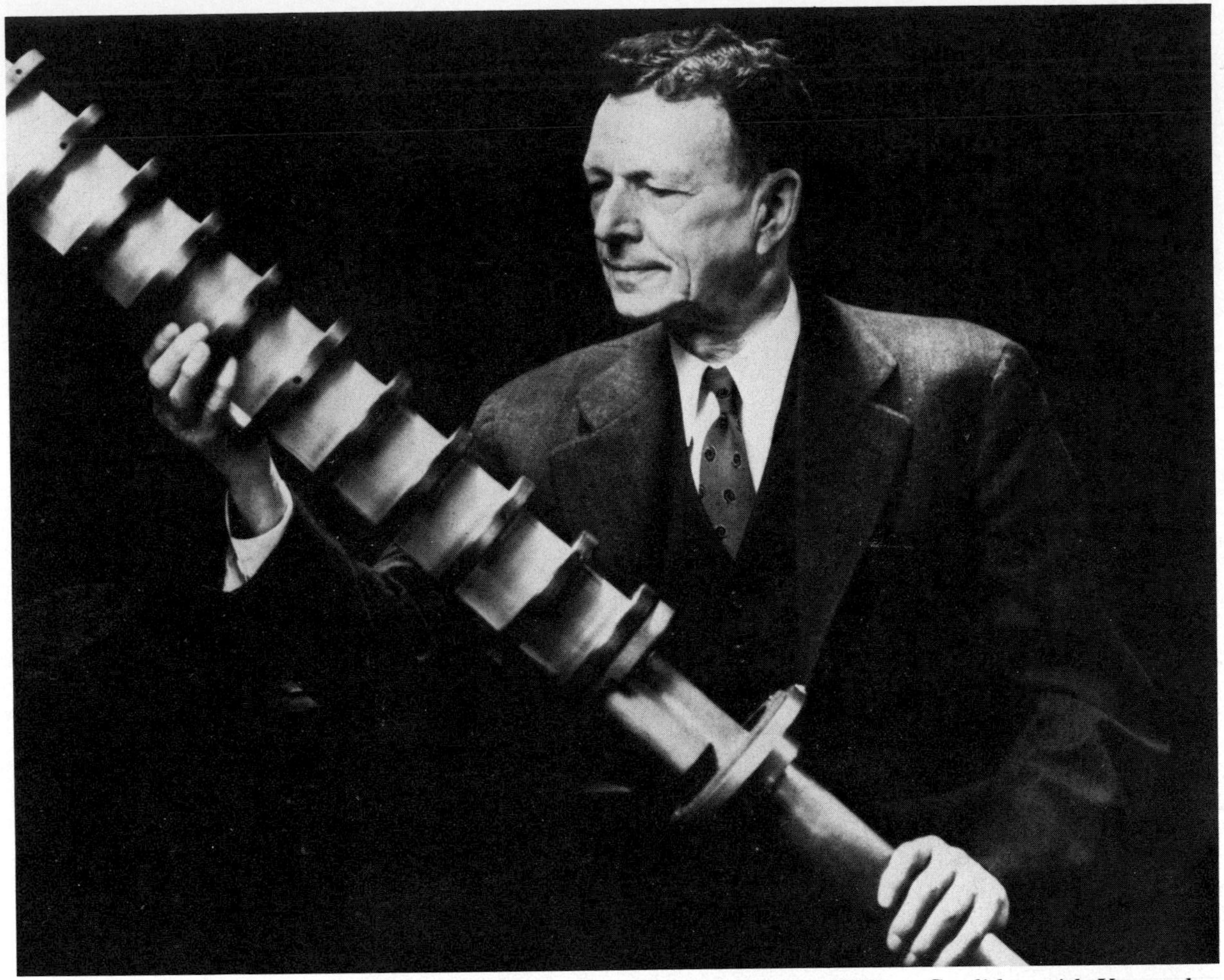

FIG. 262 *Dr. William Coolidge with Xray tube.*

setts; E. W. Rice, vice-President; Charles P. Steinmetz; and A.G. Davis, Manager of the Patent Department. The latter three were eventual residents of the Realty Plot. These men selected as the first Director Dr. Willis R. Whitney, who was a professor at the Massachusetts Institute of Technology. Dr. Whitney was at first skeptical of this concept, but he agreed to work part-time in Schenectady. Soon, he realized that research problems in industry were as challenging as those in his college laboratory, and he moved to Schenectady to devote his energies to the Research Laboratory.

The most pressing problem facing General Electric in the early years was the filament of the incandescent lamp. In 1900, Edison reportedly said of the carbon filament that it had been so perfected that it was unlikely it would ever be materially improved. This filament, however, had a short life and was too fragile for prolonged use in trains and boats because of constant jarring. Further, the carbon in the filament gradually evaporated and darkened the glass so that the lamp lost efficiency. Whitney worked on this problem for a time by himself, but in 1905 he recruited Dr. William Coolidge, his most prolific inventor and eventual successor as director in 1932. Arriving in Schenectady, Coolidge took a room at 69 Union Avenue (fig. 39). To his parents he wrote, "It is located about one and a half miles from the laboratory, and is very pleasantly situated on high ground. It is up one flight and is a southeast corner room with three nice large windows. It has gas and electricity, and a large wardrobe. A nice bathroom is nearby on the same floor. The wallpaper is in good taste. The house itself is very pretty and but two years old. It is occupied by a widow, her son, and one or two daughters. My favorable impressions of the place are probably due to the fact that one of the daughters showed me the room . . . Most of the men here advise me against going out of town so far, but the high ground appeals to me so much that I think I shall try it for awhile." Coolidge later bought a home on Lenox Road (fig. 215).

FIG. 263   Irving Langmuir (1881-1957).

Coolidge had a grounding in metallurgy, and his first assignment was the problem of the lamp filament. Whitney's idea had been to heat the carbon filament to a high temperature before installing it in a lamp to burn off the impurities that darkened the glass. The resulting filament, surprisingly, was changed by the heat to a metallic carbon that operated three times more efficiently than the original carbon filament. This "GEM" (General Electric Metalized) lamp, though brittle, was successfully marketed for twelve years.

Europeans were experimenting with metal filaments of osmium, tantalum, and tungsten. Because of their partial success, Coolidge began experimenting with tungsten filaments. Tungsten was an extremely brittle material which could not be molded into a wire. In Europe this problem was solved by mixing powdered tungsten with sugar syrup and squirting it through a hole into a thread. The thread was then heated to drive off the sugar binder. The method was unreliable, but the resulting lamp was more efficient than the GEM lamp. General Electric actually purchased the American rights to the process, but it was never used because Coolidge developed his own method of extruding tungsten powder using an amalgam of cadmium as the binder. This was the famous "Mazda" lamp, named after the Persian god of light (fig. 261). The Mazda lamp remained fragile, however, and so Coolidge next tackled the problem of making a "ductile" tungsten which could be drawn into a flexible, shock resistant wire. Two years later, he ingeniously solved this problem through a process whereby the tungsten was reworked under pressure with red-hot, steel rollers. The European scientific community was taken by surprise when Coolidge visited in 1909 with a roll of tungsten wire that could be freely shipped and handled. Dr. Blau, head of one of their largest research institutions, was at first reluctant to see Coolidge, but when he was shown the tungsten wire, he "grabbed the spool and rushed from the room, presumably to test it. When he returned, he seemed almost crazy, so much so that Coolidge

was worried lest he do harm to himself." Ductile tungsten is the basis of the modern incandescent lamp. In 1914 alone, it is estimated, its efficiency, compared to that of the older GEM lamp, saved Americans two billion dollars in electricity costs.

Many other achievements marked Dr. Coolidge's remarkable career, of which the most well known is the "Coolidge Tube," the prototype of all modern X-ray tubes. Early X-ray tubes contained a small amount of gas. As the X-ray tube heated with use, the gas pressure varied, and with it the performance of the tube. Coolidge changed the design of the tube so that it could operate as a vacuum tube without gas; he experimented taking pictures of his own hand until the hair on the back of it fell out. The Coolidge Tube achieved consistent results which changed radiology from an art to a science (fig. 262).

The early work of Irving Langmuir, who came to the Research Laboratory in 1909, dovetails with that of Coolidge. Even with ductile tungsten, lamps gradually lost efficiency as a darkening layer of evaporating tungsten vapor slowly precipitated on the glass. Coolidge had produced pure tungsten wire, so impurities were not at fault. Might not an imperfect vacuum in the bulb be the source of the problem? Researchers, suspecting this, were searching for ways to produce more perfect vacuums so that the question could be settled. Langmuir reasoned that an easier route to the answer was to study the effect of gases upon the tungsten wire. In his words: "I hoped that in this way I would become so familiar with these effects of gas that I could extrapolate to zero gas pressure, and thus predict, without really trying, how good the lamp would be if we could produce a perfect vacuum." He worked three years on this problem and came to the startling conclusion that, even in a perfect vacuum, the lamp would darken. Further work with varied gases led to a lamp filled with inert gas at atmospheric pressure which prevented the evaporation of the tungsten. Modern incandescent lamps use Langmuir's gas and Coolidge's tungsten.

FIG. 264 Early view of the Hillman house (1905), 1155 Avon Road. This design is taken from the California Bungalow-Mission tradition. The low profile of the gables and the particular way in which the wide eaves intersect the gables signal the Bungalow style. Horizontality is emphasized, not only by the thin lines of trim which divide the floors but also by the way that alternate rows of shingles have been dropped to create a banding effect.

FIG. 265 The Hillman house, postcard view, with inscription—"Electric House. Where nothing but electricity is used for light, heat, or fuel." There was some confusion in the press about the house since, by Hillman's own account, a coal furnace was necessary in the winter.

Langmuir's basic research ultimately culminated in his winning the Nobel Prize in 1932 for work in the field of surface chemistry. He postulated and proved that a single layer of gas molecules adheres to the surface of a solid or liquid, bound loosely by valency charges of the surface atoms. From this grew his theory that catalysts act by adsorbing the reacting substances onto their surfaces, where chemical reactions then occur in the adsorbed film. Although others before him made important contributions, the breadth of his work has led some to call him the "father of surface chemistry" (fig. 263). When Langmuir became the first scientist employed by an industrial laboratory to win a Nobel Prize, formal recognition was given to the importance of undirected basic research by industry.

Harry W. Hillman was head of the Electric Heating department of General Electric in 1905 when he constructed his experimental house to demonstrate new domestic applications of electricity (figs. 264-266). His interests were far more pragmatic than Langmuir's, but there is a kinship between the researcher expanding knowledge and the business man expanding markets. In 1905, houses were wired with a single circuit used exclusively for lighting. The few appliances in existence could only be used by unscrewing a lightbulb

FIG. 266 The living room of the Hillman house, 1155 Avon Road, is paneled with dark oak wainscoting and has an oak beamed ceiling.

(fig. 267). All cooking and heating employed wood or coal because of the limited capacity of the single house circuit.

Hillman conceived of a house with two circuits, one for lights and another for heating and cooking. He also envisioned placing outlets in each room so that other electrical devices could be plugged in. Was such an idea practical? His demonstration that it was generated world-wide interest. Specifications for the house were drawn in two ways; in one, a full cellar was excavated for coal and wood storage and provisions were made for a kitchen range with its inevitable chimney; in the other, only half the cellar was excavated, there was no range or chimney, and the second heating circuit was included. When estimates were examined, the extra circuit cost "only $125, or less than 1 percent of the total investment," and the amount saved by the omission of the chimney and storage cellar was enough to purchase all the electrical utensils needed for the house (figs. 268, 269). The choice of a Bungalow design was not coincidental; it was a clever architect who recognized that if Hillman wanted a "house without chimneys," he could borrow a style from a region where they were not necessary.

"The house without a kitchen chimney" was visited by Robert Crouse of the Society for Electrical Development, and a full-page story with pictures appeared in a Sunday edition of the *New York Herald*. Newspapers across the country picked up the story, and Hillman received requests for photographs from the editors of newspapers in Berlin, London, and Paris.

Five instruments in the house recorded the room temperature and power consumption during the first winter. One drawback to electric power was its high cost in the days prior to the massive generators that were to follow. Hillman responded that while the power might cost more, engineering design was making electrical appliances more efficient. In 1906 he wrote, "It is a matter of common knowledge that in the operation of boiling eggs, either with a gas stove or coal stove, a small quantity of water, say a pint, is placed in an ordi-

nary cooking utensil either on the lid of the stove or over a gas flame. Several minutes are required to bring the water to a boil, and the eggs are placed in the dish for three (or more) minutes. In comparison, the electric egg steamer requires forty-five seconds for a spoonful of water to arrive at steaming point; the cover is then raised, the eggs are dropped in. I claim that this application of electricity, as suggested by a thoughtful engineer, represents a principle of economy that affects time and labor in a way to make the experience with electricity in my home a success. This point of economy in time and expense is mentioned simply as an illustration of many new applications of electricity, bringing the cost of operation down to

FIG. 267 Interior of the earlier Hillman house on Douglas Road. Note that the table lamp is plugged into a socket of the ceiling fixture. This photograph was taken around the time that Hillman was building the Avon Road house. The furnishings are those of Mrs. George Moon who lived in the house briefly before moving to Rugby Road.

FIG. 268 The Hillman house had all the conveniences, including this electric washing machine.

FIG. 269   *Kitchen table in the Hillman house.*
The oven is on the lower shelf. Hot-plates are
plugged in above.

such an insignificant sum that people are naturally very much attracted to the devices." Regarding the use of electric heat he wrote, "I have used to advantage four luminous radiators as an electric system of heating during spring and fall seasons for auxiliary or supplemental heat. It is well known that late in September and early in October the average temperature is not such as to require starting the central heating system in the house. Still it is frequently done; then the weather changes and the fire is allowed to go out again. The cost of operation must necessarily be high. . . . With the electric auxiliary system, quick heat in the bathroom for fifteen minutes in the morning or at night is sufficient and not expensive (fig. 270)."

Hillman described his house in a paper read before the Association of Edison Electric Illuminating Companies at the Hotel Wentworth, Portsmouth, New Hampshire. Samuel Insull was present and moved that a committee of engineers verify his claims. Their recommendation was that electric heating and electrical appliances should be vigorously pushed by the member companies. Thus began the development and marketing of the refrigerators, stoves, and irons that have transformed the lives of subsequent generations.

The Martin P. Rice house, which we will next examine, symbolizes the painstaking efforts to achieve the "ideal residential development" envisioned by the Schenectady Realty Company. The "house without a kitchen chimney" is a quiet reminder of contributions to civilization by the restive minds who walked these gracious streets.

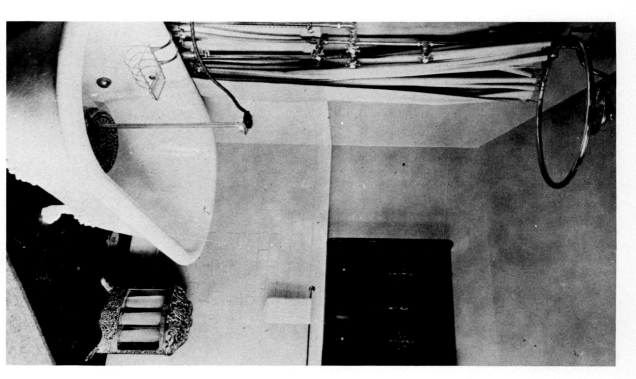

FIG. 270 *Bathroom showing one of the electric heaters, as well as an immersion heater in the bathtub!*

CHAPTER IX

The Chronicle of Martin P. Rice

Grouped in this chapter are houses of the Tudor Revival style. Although our country comprises many ethnic groups, all Americans trace a cultural heritage to England. As the Colonial Imitation style rose to dominate domestic construction in the Realty Plot, a small number of houses in the Tudor Revival style were constructed along side. By virtue of our common language with its nation of origin, the English Tudor house was not viewed as foreign as was the French Château or Italian Villa. For those seeking to eulogize their heritage, this style was an acceptable alternative to the Colonial Imitation. Another reason for the appearance of the Tudor Revival style was its similarity to the Queen Anne. Older architects, or architects who could not ascribe to the academic confinement of the Colonial Imitation, could continue to gain commissions by switching to the yet picturesque Tudor Revival. Then, too, this style, by virtue of its many gables and antique ornaments, was so inherently luxurious that it attracted any client bent upon displaying wealth. As the Colonial Imitation style waned in the 1930's, a "pseudo Tudor" style flourished. Even today, this pseudo-Tudor style, imparted by a few exposed timbers, lends that certain touch of class to uncountable tract houses.

But the Tudor Revival style did not, like Athena, spring upon the scene full grown from the head of Zeus, nor was this popular style the sole British contribution to domestic architecture. In the last chapter we saw the contribution of the English

Arts and Crafts movement to the Bungalow style; in the next chapter we will note the Modernistic influence of Voysey and the English country house. Further, the Queen Anne style had features of the Tudor even at its beginnings in the 1870's. The Ely house (1905), for instance, can be viewed as Tudor Revival or Queen Anne, and the date of construction straddles the dividing line between the two (fig. 271). Queen Anne elements are the shingled surface and the skirting-out of the second story over the first. The half-timbering in the gable is Tudor Revival, but half-timbering was common in the Queen Anne. However, the squareness of the house and its lack of other Queen Anne features—such as a polygonal bay, a tower, or a wrap-around porch—move the house away from the Victorian. Comparison of the Ely house with a pure Queen Anne building in the Realty Plot makes the antecedents of the Tudor Revival style quite clear (fig. 24).

The Frank Hoppman house (1909), 1156 Stratford Road, is somewhat later than the Ely house; with the exception of its large porch (fig. 272), it has very little surviving from the Queen Anne. Half-timbering, the symbol of 'Tudor Revival, is now the most prominent feature. The term "half-timbering" refers to a method of construction in which heavy wooden beams made up the framework of the house. Between these beams, stucco was applied over a brick fill, leaving the weight-bearing beams partially exposed. In authentically half-timbered buildings, then, the beams were stra-

FIG. 271 The William G. Ely house (1905), 1360 Lenox Road. Ely built and occupied three houses in the Realty Plot.

FIG. 272 *The Hoppman house (1909), early view.*

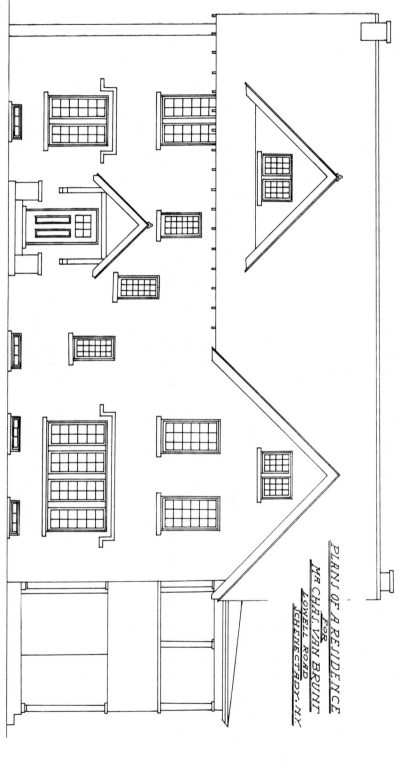

PLANS OF A RESIDENCE
FOR
MR CHAS. VAN BRUNT
LOWELL ROAD
SCHENECTADY. N.Y.

FIG. 273   *Window detail of the Hoppman house.*

FIG. 274   *Elevation of the Charles G. Van Brunt house (1913) by W.T.B. Mynderse. The house has some Bungalow features evidenced by its porch and broad, raftered eaves.*

tegically placed to perform their function of holding up the roof. In the Tudor Revival, the beams were purely decorative, so that they were invariably arranged to enhance the design. Such is the case in the Hoppman house, as the half-timbering design has been carefully worked out in reverse diagonals to complement the slope of the gables and highlight the windows. Other Tudor effects are the bargeboards, the facing boards on the eaves, and the bands of trim over the first floor windows, called "label moldings" (fig. 273).

In the Van Brunt house (1913), 1436 Lowell Road, a Tudor Revival inflection is imparted by the delicate label moldings over the windows and by the prominent medieval chimney with its offsets (figs. 274, 275). The plaster work not only anticipates the English country house but is also authentic for the Tudor style, as it was common to totally conceal the beam framework of a Tudor structure with plaster. The broad eaves are not Tudor but were borrowed from the Bungalow style; they serve the necessary function of keeping water from running down the plaster. In the mild coastal European climate, broad eaves were not needed, and early Dutch and English houses were built without them. The first settlers tried to use the same techniques, but in our harsh climate, water ran down the plaster wall and froze. The ice expanded and cracked the plaster. Early builders quickly learned their lesson and broadened the eaves; however, the colonial plaster was still not durable enough. Ultimately, stucco was abandoned until superior materials allowed its reintroduction during the period we have been considering. Charles G. Van Brunt graduated from Harvard in 1893 and did graduate work at the Massachusetts Institute of Technology. In 1905 he joined the staff of the Research Laboratory, where he organized the

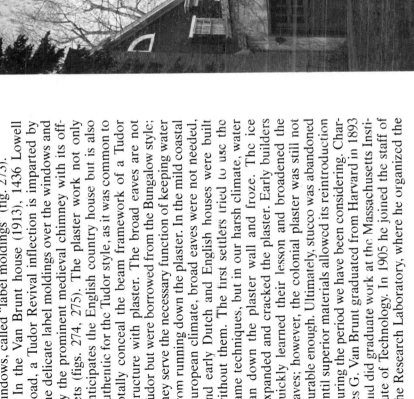

FIG. 275 Street façade of the Van Brunt house. With wide eaves, rambling asymmetry, label moldings, and plastered exterior, Mynderse has blended elements of the Bungalow, Tudor Revival, and English Country style in this design.

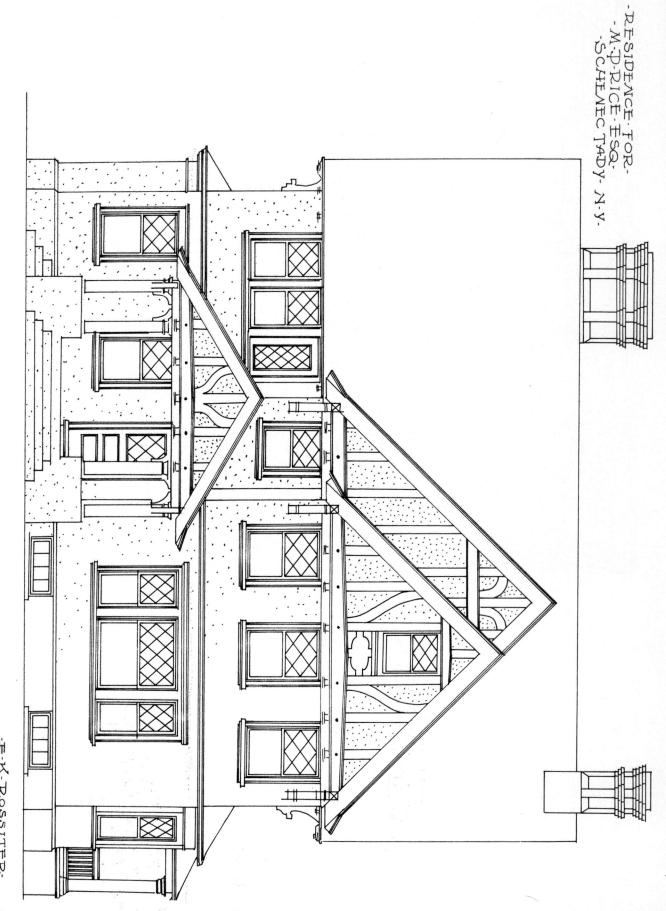

·RESIDENCE·FOR·
·M·P·RICE·ESQ·
·SCHENECTADY·N·Y·

·FRONT·ELEVATION·

·E·K·ROSSITER·
·ARCHITECT·
·15·WEST·38th·ST·N·Y·C·

FIG. 276 Front elevation of the Martin P. Rice
house (1912) by E.K. Rossiter.

FIG. 277 M.P. Rice house. Rice enlarged the house in the 1930's.

Analytical Chemistry division. He is best remembered for his work in microchemistry. He pioneered the techniques that permitted analysis of minute quantities of unknown substances. Using these techniques, he was able to study the way in which electrical currents are transferred in sliding contacts. As all electric motors employ such contacts, this work was fundamental to their design.

The best example of Tudor Revival in the Realty Plot is the Martin P. Rice house (1912), 1255 Lowell Road (figs. 276-278). Half-timbering was used to accent various areas, but the architect was very careful to place the timbers so that we would not be misled into thinking they have structural significance. (Notice their use over the porch where such heavy supports would not be necessary, and notice, too, their absence in other areas.) Old-fashioned, wide, Queen Anne windows were used with a diamond pattern to suggest medieval windows. There is more use of intricate gabling than we have so far seen.

Martin P. Rice was the brother of Edwin Wilbur Rice, President of General Electric, and the uncle of Chester Rice. He was Manager of the Publication Bureau of General Electric from 1897 until his retirement in 1932; he also managed General Electric Broadcasting. In these positions he supervised the opening of WGY in Schenectady in 1922; KGO in Oakland, California, in 1924; and KOA in Denver, Colorado, in 1924. He supervised all publicity, advertising, printing, and photography for the company. As Manager of broadcasting, he presided over many notable broadcasts, such as Admiral Byrd's from Antarctica, and he introduced to radio audiences many prominent people including Charles Lindbergh and Amelia Earhart (fig. 279).

Martin P. Rice was a frugal man who kept files of all his correspondence. Thus, a nearly complete picture is preserved of the interplay between Rice and his New York architect, E.K. Rossiter (fig. 280). Though it becomes apparent that Rice had his eccentricities, the subdued reactions of those who came in contact with him suggest that his high expectations for his house were the norm for this period. Rice knew of Rossiter because the

FIG. 278 *M.P. Rice house, detail.*

FIG. 279 *Martin P. Rice (d. 1950) was responsible for developing the company's broadcasting policies and advocated that the new media should transmit drama, news, and classical music.*

latter had designed George Emmons's house ten years earlier (fig. 332). On February 4, 1911, he wrote to Rossiter, "The English cottage suggested itself without any very systematic reasoning. My idea is to have a small house that is distinctive, yet comfortable and in good taste. I particularly dislike 'freak' houses." (He did not, unfortunately, further typify a "freak" house). Both men agreed that the house would be located on the lot to take maximum advantage of the view of the ravine. One difficulty was the New York location of E.K. Rossiter. Rice, naturally, did not want to pay travel expenses for Rossiter for frequent visits to Schenectady, but he also worried that, with too few visits, there would be inadequate supervision of the job windows, he requested that "small square or diamond-shaped panes be used in the upper sash, and large panes in the lower sash. Possibly leaded glass could be used in the large window in the stairway hall. I think all windows should be so low that a person sitting in an ordinary chair can readily see out." His comments confirm what we have noted elsewhere; the broad Queen Anne window was popular and practical and was retained in later styles.

After this congenial start, a major obstacle surfaced in April of 1911 which delayed construction for one year. Wrote Rice on April 19, 1911, "You will recall that my lot lies to the north of a ravine with a narrow strip of level land intervening. For the past ten years the ravine property has been considered private, and owners of abutting land have been permitted to cultivate the intervening strip, and guard it against public trespass. The Realty Company recently resolved to construct a walk along the edge of the ravine close to my southern boundary, and on the same level. As this walk would undoubtedly become a general thoroughfare, it would rob my property of its privacy," which was a deciding feature in its purchase." Opposition to the walkway caused the Directors of the Realty Company to forestall their plans, but throughout 1911, no further action was taken formally to accept or abandon the proposal, leaving Rice with a set of unused drawings. Rossiter sympathized with him in December: "I notice that human nature is the same all over the world and the things that we cannot take a personal interest in move more slowly than where the want is keenly felt, and as the Directors who have the settling of these matters are only indirectly interested they proceed with the usual indifference." Rice forwarded these remarks to brother Wilbur, and the next day, he was invited to attend a board meeting where it was agreed that he could purchase the land adjoining the ravine.

Correspondence resumed in January, 1912, and plans were finalized to begin construction. Rice suggested substituting tile for a slate roof as tile was cheaper; he also asked Rossiter's opinion of small square panes in the upper sash of the windows. Rossiter replied, "I should very much prefer using a tile roof to one of slate." He submitted an estimate from the Ludowici-Celadon Company of $650 for applying shingle tile, "French pattern." "The price seems to me a very reasonable one and when you consider the imperishable nature of the material, I believe that you can add far more to the value of the house than the difference between this and applying shingles as called for. If you apply tile it would be folly not to line the gutters and flash the chimneys with copper. In other words, we should build this roof as the Deacon built his one-horse shay, making no one part stronger than another." In the matter of the window panes "diamond panes on the whole are more characteristic than the square ones [which] seem to me to belong more to the Colonial than to the English domestic."

Rice commented on a wide range of small details as construction progressed. At one point he asked about the practicality and cost of installing a laundry chute from the second-floor bathroom to the cellar with an opening in the kitchen. Rossiter wrote that a metal chute costing about ten dollars could be incorporated, but he advised against an opening in the kitchen for, "if the door to the chute in the kitchen were not absolutely tight, it would act as a vent flue in the bathroom and you would be informed long in advance of the meal hour what the menu was for breakfast." Replied Rice: "On further consideration I think it would be as well to omit the laundry chute. It would probably not be used enough to pay for the space it occupies." The present owner comments, "You can tell he was a bachelor!" He questioned the use of veneer doors, oak on the outside and birch on the inside, instead of solid oak or ash. Would the outside doors withstand the elements? Rossiter answered, "As far as I am aware they never make nowadays doors of solid oak or ash, for they are very apt to warp, and when they do they defy all known processes to bring them back into shape. Indeed there is an innate depravity about doors made without a veneer that will in comparison

FIG. 280 E.K. Rossiter (1854-1941). His book (co-authored with F.A. Wright) Modern House Painting, (1883), has become a standard reference work of Victorian color schemes.

as it progressed. A compromise was struck that Rossiter would schedule visits "so well-timed as to make unnecessary a large number." Rice, meanwhile, would follow the day-to-day progress of the project.

Initially, the design phase proceeded smoothly. Rice was careful to insist that only General Electric products be used—"I would certainly subject myself to a great deal of criticism if I equipped my house with a competitor's appliances." The double-wiring system pioneered by H.W. Hillman was employed—"As we have a special rate for electricity used for heating and cooking, I wish to run a separate circuit to the kitchen, dining room and laundry for toasters, flat irons, etc." (fig. 281). For

FIG. 281 *Rice's department produced a promotional film,* The Home Electrical *which extolled the virtues of electric appliances. His house was the backdrop. Here we see professional actors arriving in an electric car and using his central vacuum system.*

leave any specimen of human nature an almost perfect angel to reckon with. I have never known of well-veneered doors to go back on their maker as human beings oft do."

Woodwork, fireplace mantels, hardware, lighting fixtures, and wallpaper were the subjects of dozens of letters through the spring and summer of 1912. Rice submitted his own sketches for custom-made hardware and lighting fixtures. Always cost conscious, he decided not to build a garage—"The garage plans are much too elaborate for the present condition of my pocketbook." Later he felt he could reduce costs by designing the garage himself; but he finally relented when

Rossiter agreed to do the work for a nominal sum and when he learned that construction at a later time would cost even more. "In working up the interior of the house, kindly bear in mind that I am partial to rather plain and simple effects," wrote Rice on April 6, 1912. The first designs for fireplaces were "too elaborate for my quiet tastes. I would be glad to see such mantels occasionally in a friend's house; perhaps you could modify them by omitting the sunbursts and borders. I have sketched very roughly two mantels from my brother's house, which are always pleasing and satisfactory." Two days later Rossiter defended his choice. "This is a copy of an old mantel that was brought over from Ireland, and will not be out of keeping with the interior of your house. It is dignified and simple and worthwhile holding on to." By return mail: "How would it do to take the mantel originally designed for the den and use it in the living room with such modifications as may be required[?] I am really quite pleased with the den mantel, but I

cannot quite bring myself to see the appropriateness of the living room mantel, and I have a constitutional objection to sunbursts. If we could have the Old English for the den, and use the original den mantel for either the living room or the second-story chamber, I feel as though the final result would be much more satisfactory." The ever-deferential architect eventually sorted out the mantels to his patron's satisfaction (fig. 282).

There were times of trauma—"Will you please reserve for me three or four rolls of paper like the attached? Yesterday one of the paperers became intoxicated, and spoiled several pieces of paper before it was noticed"—and a misunderstanding over the design of the stairway was termed Rice's *Bête Noire.* Not wanting to extend the stairway

FIG. 282 *Living room fireplace of the M.P. Rice house.*

too far into the hall while at the same time wanting to use a standard height door into a bathroom under the landing, Rossiter had added an extra riser in the stair. The landing was thus ten inches narrower, requiring the omission of a window seat. "It was simply a case of 'Robbing Peter to pay Paul.' On the whole, the gain that has come about by these slight adjustments is greater it seems to me than the loss that has been sustained." But Rice lamented, "It reminds me just a little of some of the successful surgical operations in which the patient has the poor grace to die. Of course, my case is not so serious, but it looks as if I would have to be content to amputate the window seat and then pay for considerable millwork that will be discarded."

Work was completed in June of 1913 at a total cost of $15,666.

Dear Mr. Rossiter:

Permit me at this time to express my hearty appreciation of your designs for the house, and of your careful and patient over-seeing of all the details of construction. All I can say about the finished work is that it is even more satisfactory than I had anticipated. If you are willing to let me have one of your recent photographs, I would be very glad to have it framed and give it a place in one of the rooms of the house because I think it is quite appropriate that visitors who inspect the building should also have an opportunity to know something about the designer.

Very truly yours,

Martin P. Rice

Martin P. Rice

Dear Mr. Rice:

I have received your letter of yesterday's date enclosing check for the balance of the account. I don't know whether I am more pleased with your flattering testimonial or with the cash, both of which are most acceptable. I think, however, that if anyone is entitled to wear a crown to designate the virtue of patience you are that individual rather than myself.

Knowing that you were obliged to take a sea trip in order to restore your nerves that became inflamed through errors that befell the staircase, I feel you are particularly generous in wishing my photograph. Try and carry me in happy remembrance without a souvenir of this kind for modesty forbids me to parade my features to your admiring friends. I think it is Shakespeare who remarks: "Happy is he who learns of his distractions and sets them to mending." You may be very sure that this mishap on the staircase will remain the individual instance of miscalculation. With all good wishes which do not exclude the thought of somebody sharing this home with you in due time, I am,

Yours very truly,

E.K. Rossiter

E.K. Rossiter

The chronicle of Martin P. Rice documents the incredible industry devoted to erecting this dwelling for a lone occupant, but the other houses of the Realty Plot are proof that such personal investment was not unique. There is a richness in this inventory of private correspondence which reflects the gentility of a time which is at once within living memory for a few and forever beyond reach for all.

Wendell Avenue, Schenectady.

220

FIG. 283 *The Armstrong house (c. 1901) (on the left) in an early postcard view of Wendell Avenue. The First Unitarian Society has replaced the Emmons house on the right.*

CHAPTER X

Modernism

A dissertation on Modern architecture would be well beyond the scope of this book. Furthermore, the reader of a book of this type might be intrinsically less interested in this subject. Nonetheless, since there are nearly a score of houses in the Realty Plot that anticipate contemporary design, some explanation is necessary. Early in this book, architectural history was drastically condensed to orient the reader; we will follow the same course now.

There are two fundamental features of Modern architecture which separate it from earlier periods. The first is an overwhelming concern for "space." Twentieth-century design was heavily influenced by Frank Lloyd Wright, who visualized the frame of the house as a shell which enclosed and defined an inner space. To him, walls functioned not as barriers but as screens. Rejecting Colonial Revival symmetry, Wright believed that a building should not be constructed along some preconceived geometrical plan, but should grow around convenient living or work areas. His ideas were not new. Early Victorians had similarly reacted against Greek Revival. Though they did not phrase it quite as Wright would, the Victorian utilized space to achieve pleasing visual effects. A bay window or a tower, after all, enclosed space. Wright's designs were descendants of the Victorian ethic, and he was influenced by Henry Hobson Richardson, the great American originator of the Queen Anne style. However, Wright modified Richardson's concern for space by forsaking picturesque design.

Though Wright was concerned with aesthetics, he sought to include only those spaces which were functional; no functionless towers and no frilly ornaments were incorporated into his designs. His impact has been remarkable because contemporary society agrees that the primary function of a building is to enclose usable space. One concrete example will suffice for illustration of this point. The suburban tract house does not attract buyers because of any political statement it makes or because of an appealing design. It sells itself on the basis of its low maintenance and its convenient arrangement of rooms—an attached garage, a "family room," a "step-saver" kitchen, a patio—all features first dramatized by Frank Lloyd Wright.

The second hallmark of the Modern style is its avoidance of any historical reference. The glass skyscraper is devoid of Palladian windows. The skyscraper is mentioned intentionally as this building form developed at the end of the nineteenth century and was recognized as something which had never been seen before. Louis Sullivan, the first architect deliberately to seek a new design for the new building, and Frank Lloyd Wright were intent that the new forms for the new age would draw no inspiration from what they considered the tired ideas of the past. Parallel developments were occurring in art and music, and the technological developments of the twentieth century can leave no doubt that we live in a different time from that of our grandfathers. In the Realty Plot we find no chrome-and-glass homes, and at first

FIG. 284 *The William H. Winslow house, River Forest, Illinois, (1893) by Frank Lloyd Wright.*

FIG. 285 *The Ernst Berg house (1913).*

glance the houses in this chapter might seem more logically grouped under other headings. But just as H.G. Wells described his futuristic time machine as having ornate, Victorian filigree, so the architects expressed Modern concepts in designs which superficially resemble those discussed in preceding chapters.

That Frank Lloyd Wright influenced building design is evident in the Albert Armstrong house (c. 1902), 1203 Wendell Avenue (fig. 283). The house, with its formal symmetry and hipped roof, is related to the Colonial Revival style; but here the roof is lower pitched, and the broad eaves act as a unifying umbrella over the house. Broad windows are tucked directly beneath the eaves, and there are no references to any Colonial period; the complete effect is similar to that of Wright's Winslow house in River Forest, Illinois (fig. 284).

The Ernst J. Berg house (1913), 1336 Lowell Road, with its correct segmental Georgian pediment surmounting the entrance, is closely allied to the Colonial Imitation style (fig. 285). Symmetry is lacking as the door has been pushed to one side to make room for a bay window. The arrangement of dormers, doors, and windows are anything but haphazard, but just as certainly violates the order of the Colonial Imitation. The architect and owner arrived at this scheme to fulfill some requirement of the owner in laying out the floor plan. Enough Colonial detailing was used to create the proper feeling of a Colonial style, but functional considerations took control of the rest of the design. The same considerations dominate the design of the Haigh-Salmon house (1915) two doors away (figs. 286, 287). The architect would have been well aware that this house was historically impossible. Shutters on the windows and a Federal style porch give the house a weak colonial voice, but otherwise the four openings do not work

DEL. B. SALMON

FIG. 287 Haigh sold the house in 1917 to Del B. Salmon, who was the youngest man to be caricatured in Schenectady Just For Fun. While serving as Assistant Corporation Counsel from 1906 to 1909, he rewrote the City's building code.

FIG. 286 The Haigh-Salmon house (1915), 1284 Lowell Road, by W.T.B. Mynderse.

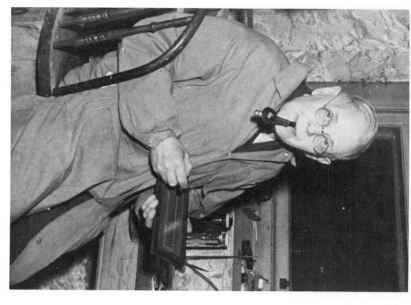

FIG. 288 Dr. Ernst Berg (1871-1941).

FIG. 289 Early view of the Robert Maxon house (1939), the last house built in the Realty Plot during the life of the Schenectady Realty Company.

together to make any powerful design statement. In both these homes, concern for interior space, a nascent Modernism, dictated emphasis of building use over adherence to a strict design.

Dr. Ernst Berg was for nearly thirty years the Chairman of the Department of Engineering at Union College. He assisted Charles Steinmetz in preparation of the book, *Theory Calculation of Alternating Current*, and later authored several books of his own, including *Electric Energy* (1908), *Electric Engineering* (1915), and *Heaviside's Operational Calculus*. These books were standard texts in most electrical engineering courses. Berg was also a radio pioneer and inventor. In 1916 he produced the first two-way voice program in the United States. Berg bestowed a legacy of generosity and friendship to generations of students. In

tribute, Union President Dixon Ryan Fox said his contribution "to the Union College community, the City of Schenectady, and the world of science is beyond easy computation. His mind touched the thought of mathematicians and engineers throughout this continent and others. His heart touched the life of innumerable students who passed under his friendly direction" (fig. 288).

In some instances, Modern architecture has produced dramatic works of art which remain concerned with function. In others, the house may cease to make a strong architectural statement

224

FIG. 291 *The Albert Boynton house (1924), 1477 Lowell Road.*

and become instead an amorphous collection of building materials. The Robert C. Maxon residence (1939), 1122 Nott Street, incorporates a Tudor style half-timber design on its right side while employing a vaguely colonial design for the main block of the house on the left (fig. 289). Ambiguity as to which of the doors is the main entrance results from its construction as a combined home and office (fig. 290). The Albert Boynton house (1924) also shows a loss of concern for style (fig. 291). Admittedly, this house was not built on as grand a scale as some of the earlier houses, but this does not entirely explain the finished product. The eaves are similar to those used in the Bungalow style. The door retains the classic tall-tall-short Federal paneling, but the

FIG. 290 *Dr. Robert Maxon, a physician, practiced only briefly in the house. He died during World War II.*

225

FIG. 292 *The Brown School (1905), 1184 Rugby Road.*

FIG. 293 *The Elmer Avenue School (1905).*

porch design makes no real historical allusion. If anything, it reminds one of a Spanish Colonial archway from the Cameron house (fig. 157). These houses exemplify a new preoccupation with "livability" over what the house "says." While this may have represented a degeneration from an artistic sense, it was evolutionary in a social sense. Concepts of Nationalism and Romanticism had been challenged by the carnage of World War I. New prosperity and mobility in this country loosened whatever class structure had existed. If houses built during this period fail to "say" anything, it is in part because the owner was uncertain exactly what he should be saying.

Modernism in the form of a desire for clean lines may not be immediately apparent. The Brown School (1905) is actually strikingly modern in its design (fig. 292). The basic motifs—the shingle surface and medieval mullion and transom windows—came from the Queen Anne style; but the building is totally lacking in any ornamentation and relies for its design entirely upon an abstract arrangement of windows grouped in bands across the exterior. Contrast this structure with a public school of the same period which has nationalistic motifs suitable for instilling patriotism in young minds (fig. 293). Unnoticed at first, there is a basic asymmetry as windows are placed to suit the interior arrangement of space. Even though the entrance is off-center, balance is achieved as window groups balance each other across the central axis. Modernism was possible here as this was an institutional building. For his home, a wealthy patron would have insisted upon something fancier.

The Brown School was established in 1893 in a house on Liberty Street. As part of the planned community, the Schenectady Realty Company encouraged Helen Brown to relocate on Rugby Road by donating the land to her. Until recent

FIG. 295 *Helen Brown.*

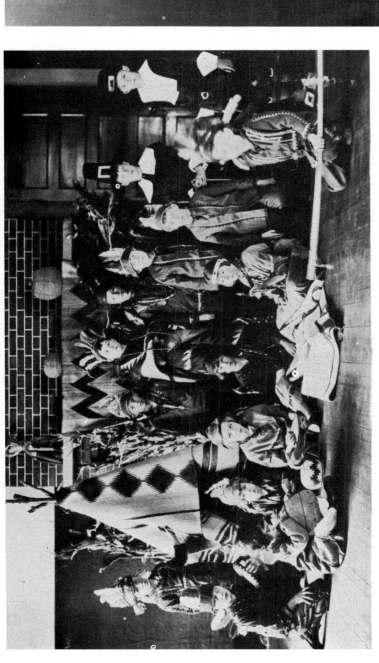

FIG. 294 *Thanksgiving pageant, date unknown.*

years, the school did in fact have the responsibility for the education of children of the Realty Plot (fig. 294). Truly, Miss Brown imposed her will when the school was built; the most important thing to her was the training that would go on inside, not the frill outside (fig. 295).

The unadorned façade of the Edward Waters house (1914), 1248 Wendell Avenue, is similar to the Brown School (fig. 296). The house is presently partially concealed behind trees, but when new, it presented a stark functionalism in contrast to the Queen Anne style house next door. Brick construction and a copper roof over the porch were enough to proclaim that a lack of ornament was not due to a lack of money; the neat little entrance lends a fashionable hint of colonial fla-

vor to the building. Interestingly, the austere front belied what was in the rear, where a Greek Revival style doorway served as entrance into the garden. The private area that the Waters family enjoyed provides sharp contrast to what the public viewed, and this was in keeping with a Modern philosophy of the primacy of individual comfort (fig. 297).

The work of C.F.A. Voysey, an English architect who was a contemporary of Frank Lloyd Wright, bridged the Modern movement and the English Arts and Crafts movement. To review his design concepts would be to iterate the views of Wright, but his designs are somewhat different because his craft grew from a foundation in the English Queen Anne style. Voysey's early works for wealthy patrons of a large firm employed half-timbering in the Tudor fashion as well as multiple roof gables. When he began to work independently, he moved to designs which limited the gables to

228

·MR·E·G·WATERS··SCHENECTADY·N·Y·
·FRONT·ELEVATION·· SCALE·1/4·INCH = 1·FOOT·
·ALFRED·BUSSELLE·ARCHT·· 132·MADISON·AVE·N·Y·C·

FIG. 296   Front elevation of the Waters house
(1914).

keep costs down while still permitting large interior spaces. His houses, emphasizing clean lines, were enormously influential and conveyed an affluent but not gaudy feeling for the English Country house (fig. 298). It is natural that Voysey's influence should seep into the Realty Plot, although his similarity to Wright makes it difficult to quantify his impact.

The use of plaster on the exterior of houses in the Realty Plot derives from English sources, and Voysey was a foremost advocate of this neutral material. The plans of the George P. Whittlesey house (1911), by New York architect Ekin Wallach, are entitled a "Plaster Country House," which clearly points at Voysey (fig. 299). There is a deliberate neutrality to the building, and its "L" floor plan affords maximum convenience to the owner. The Roy C. Muir house (1925) resembles the Whittlesey house, even to sharing an "L" plan with an off-set street gable (figs. 300, 301). Again, the plaster surface brings to mind an English Country house; however, Federal detailing has intruded in the doorway, the porch, and the fanlight high in the gable. With these motifs, the house clings slightly to the Colonial Imitation, but the voice of any particular historical period is weak, and exact classification is not possible. The house must be viewed as an expression of the Modernism we have been discussing; the internal arrangement of space or even the gradual slope of the building lot pushed aside concerns for any rigid design system.

Voysey's influence is even more evident in the Emmet-McNaughton house (1914), 1151 Lowell Road (fig. 302, 303). W.T.B. Mynderse surveyed this site and told his family that he wanted to copy another house he had seen to take advantage of the corner location, but that he was fearful the owner would reject the design. To his surprise the owner did not; and, although we do not know what antecedent he had in mind, the house Voysey built for his father bears a striking resemblance. True to the Modern spirit, there is no sharp historical reference of any kind, and the symmetrically projecting wings create a marvelously unconventional floor plan (fig. 304).

FIG. 297 *Rear of the Waters house. The occupants have turned inward in response to the accelerating bustle of the twentieth century. Contrast this with the street-facing Victorian porches of earlier years.*

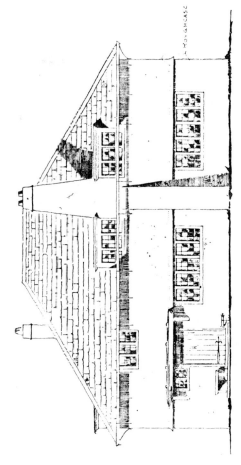

FIG. 298 *"An Artist's Cottage" by C.F.A. Voysey (1891).*

229

FIG. 299 *The George Whittlesey house (1911), 1412 Lowell Road. Whittlesey also built an earlier house on Nott Street (fig. 126). The porch vestibule is a later addition.*

FIG. 300 The Roy C. Muir house (1925), 1112 Avon Road.

FIG. 301   Roy C. Muir (1882-1973) held many executive posts in the General Electric Company during his forty-five years of service. At the time of his retirement he was General Manager of the Apparatus Department, but he soon abandoned retirement to become General Manager of the then-new Nucleonics Department.

FIG. 303   The Emmet-McNaughton house.

232

FIG. 302 The Emmet-McNaughton house (1914) has hints of the medieval English Tudor style in its overhanging second story and the chimneys which interrupt the roof line. Such chimneys are common to the Bungalow style and the English Country style.

FIG. 304 Floor plan of the Emmet-McNaughton house by W.T.B. Mynderse.

Herman LeRoy Emmet was the great-great-great-grandnephew of Robert Emmet, "the ideal patriot of the Irish Race" who was executed in Dublin in 1803. His uncle was William LeRoy Emmet, famed General Electric engineer who pioneered in the development of electric ship drives and the mercury turbine process of power generation. Herman LeRoy Emmet was Production Manager of the General Electric plant in Schenectady from 1920 to 1929; he then moved to Erie, Pennsylvania, to be works manager there.

He occupied this house only until 1918, when his growing family required relocation to an even larger house that once stood on the present site of the Y.W.C.A. on Washington Avenue. The house then passed to Archibald McNaughton, one-time President of the Clark Whitbeck Company, whose family has owned it to the present day.

Another Mynderse design, the Ely house (1924), defies exact classification. Suffice it to say that the interesting combination of intersecting gables, broad eaves, and Gothic motifs makes this a strikingly original piece of architecture (figs. 305, 306). The roof is composed of individual copper shingles, which is unique for the Realty Plot. Broad eaves interrupted by a prominent chimney were a motif of the Bungalow style and English Country house; both styles drew this design from picturesque, medieval chimneys. The flat plaster surface of the house earns its inclusion with the English Country style. Gothic detailing was expressed on the inside with pointed arches in the stairway and the cabinetry (fig. 307).

The Woodall house (1923), 1109 Adams Road, again reflected the English Country style of Voysey (fig. 308). Asymmetrically placed windows across the façade are reminiscent of the Brown School and reinforce the close tie between the English Country house and Modern architecture. Here, there are obvious Bungalow overtones in the supports under broad eaves. The lattice work is original, and when covered with vines, it would mimic the "hairy" effect of a cottage one might encounter on a quiet English side road.

Dr. Charles Woodall, born the son of a missionary in China, was a remarkable man. In his profession, he was a noted surgeon who was not only President of the County Medical Society but also Chief of Staff of Ellis Hospital. He hosted a daily radio program on medicine in the early days of radio, and he wrote two books on medicine. In his leisure time, he was an avid golfer and won the championship of the Mohawk Golf Club in 1941. He and his wife were proficient figure skaters. They skated at the official opening of Central Park as well as in competitions as far away as Pittsfield,

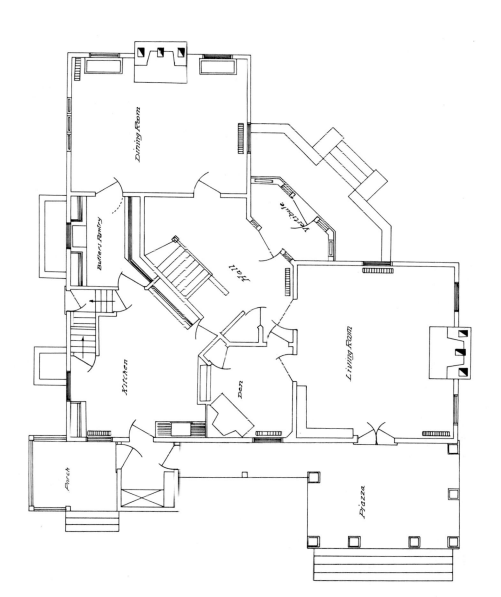

234

FIG. 305 The William G. Ely house (1924),
1141 Adams Road.

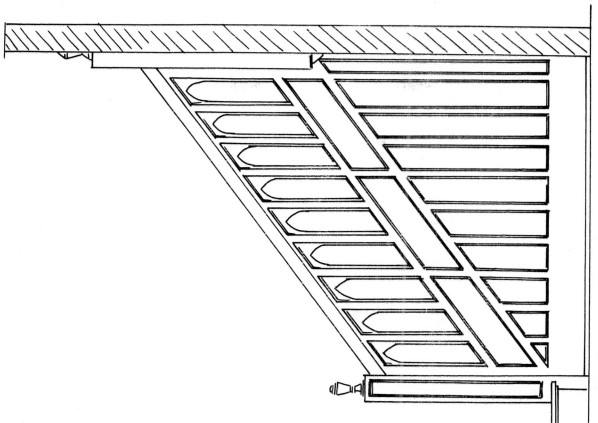

FIG. 307 *Stairway detail of the Ely house by W.T.B. Mynderse.*

STAIR · ELEVATION

FIG. 306 *The William G. Ely house.*

FIG. 309 *Dr. and Mrs. Woodall skating at Central Park, Schenectady.*

FIG. 308 *The Dr. Charles Woodall house (1923).*

Massachusetts (fig. 309), Dr. Woodall, who hand-crafted much of his own furniture, personally designed the Adams Road home. The fireplace is Adam style, copied from a photograph of a similar one in the Metropolitan Museum (fig. 310).

To the houses considered so far, we now add a group more carefully clinging to the motifs of the past while striving to make a Modern statement. It is quite likely that the architect was consciously experimenting with new forms while holding close enough to accepted conventions to retain his client.

The Charles Langley house (c. 1904), 8 Douglas Road, follows Colonial Revival lines (figs. 311, 312). The hipped roof, the central dormer, the rock-faced masonry in the foundation, the very beautiful Roman brick, the Victorian-style entrance with double-leafed doors and beveled glass—all of these are familiar elements of the style. But here, an intense symmetry conveys a feeling of immense power. The asymmetrically-placed bay regularly appears somewhere on every Colonial Revival building, and its extension through two stories is a common Victorian motif. Here, two bays have been flattened out against the building and extended upward through two stories. The entrance, so often offset in the Colonial Revival, is centrally placed, and the wide eaves are reminiscent of the Armstrong house (fig. 282). The elements of the house are all so familiar, but their combination is unique. The architect was deliberately experimenting with symmetry, not to echo some Federal or Georgian house, but to achieve a new effect.

Like the Langley house, the Thomas C. Brown house (1907) and the Langmuir house (1906) were designed by architects who were manipulating the Colonial Revival style under the influence of the Modern school (figs. 313-315). In the Langmuir house, there is a paucity of references to the Queen Anne or Colonial Revival. The Brown house does

have a number of colonial ornaments, exaggerated Federal keystones over the windows, paired,
Doric columns on the porch, and a Georgian design
in the dormer. Neither originally had shuttered
windows. Shutters, so frequently used in the colonial styles, were omitted in an impulse to Modernism.[12] Neither has multipaned windows; instead,
broad windows that could be considered the fore-
runners of modern "picture windows" were employed. The fine mortar joints and smooth-textured
brick serve much the same function as stucco in
reducing the walls to a neutral plane. Terra cotta
panels, symmetrically placed in the second story
of the Brown house, show how the architect deliberately used familiar Victorian motifs in a bizarre
way. The floating placement of these floral panels,
which were popular in the 1880's, is at odds with
their usual position tied in with the eaves, under
windows, or in bands to divide stories (fig. 316). In
summary, these houses resemble abstract pieces
of Modern architecture.

Many of the same comments apply to the J.C.
Hardie residence (1912), 1352 Lowell Road (figs.
317-319). The tile roof might suggest a Spanish
influence, but this material was used on all styles
of houses in the Realty Plot for its durable quali-
tites; nothing else of Spanish inflection can be
seen. The use of small mullion and transom windows recalls medieval forms, and such windows
were favored by the English Arts and Crafts
movement. Other elements drawn from various
pre-World War I styles occur in the broad porch
and Federal-style keystones over the windows. But
the overwhelming feeling of the house is one of
quiet, neutral symmetry; there is no other period
in which this house could have been built than the
twentieth century.

Yet another instance in which fashionable components of the period were used in unconventional
ways is the John Parker house (1909), 1188 Lowell
Road (fig. 320). A gambrel roof spreads over the
house with a large central gable facing the street.
The building looks quite balanced around the
semicircular window in the gable, but this gable is
actually slightly off-center in relation to the ground

FIG. 310   The fireplace of the Woodall house as
well as the rocker to its left were crafted by
the owner.

[12]The aluminum shutters of the Langmuir house are a recent
addition as they are obviously too small for the windows.

FIG. 311 *The Charles Langley house (c. 1904).*

FIG. 313   The Irving Langmuir house (1906),
1176 Stratford Road. Langmuir was the fourth
owner of this house that was built for Charles F.
Reynolds, a druggist. Tradition, the stature of
Langmuir, and a bronze plaque from the Department of the Interior (bolted to the brick) have
conspired to deny Reynolds his due recognition
as original occupant.

FIG. 312   Entrance of the Langley house.

FIG. 314   The Thomas C. Brown house (1907),
1174 Lowell Road.

FIG. 316 *Terracotta panel on the Brown house.*

TOM C. BROWN

FIG. 315 *Thomas C. Brown in Schenectady Just For Fun. Brown was part owner of the Brown and Lowe construction company and a state senator for three terms, serving as the Chairman of the Senate Committee of Penal Institutions.*

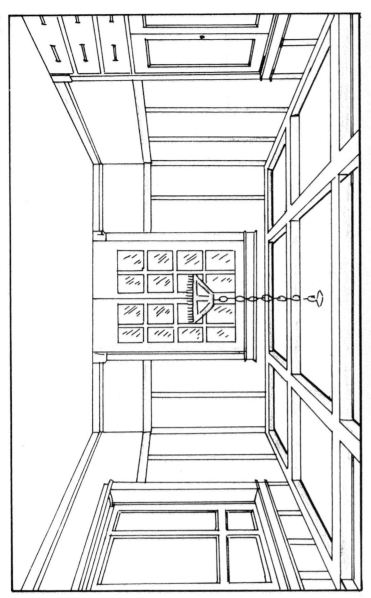

FIG. 319 The J.C. Hardie house by W.E. Stephans. There is a decided Bungalow inflection in this house, as evidenced by the architect's rendering of the dining room.

FIG. 317 Early photograph of the Hardie house (1912).

FIG. 318　Contemporary view of the Hardie house.

243

FIG. 320   The John Parker house (1909). High porch piers are taken from the Bungalow style; the squat, Doric columns on the piers have no mates in the District.

floor. Like Frank Lloyd Wright, the architect experimented here with mass and space. The first floor retreats on the right, creating a space, a sheltered porch; balanced against this, the first floor projects to the left in a large bay. There is a kinship with thrusting, cantilevered creations (such as are evident at the Empire State Mall in Albany) (figs. 321, 322).

A later owner was Chester Lang, who succeeded Martin Rice in 1932 as Manager of Advertising and Broadcasting for General Electric. Later still, he managed sales for the giant Apparatus Department, responsible for the company's business with public utilities, industry, and government agencies. In civic affairs he was a board member of Ellis Hospital for thirty-five years and its President for ten. He was on the Board of Regents of the State University of New York for four years until his untimely death in 1961.

Last in this group is the Charles DeHart Bower house (1910), built for an electrical engineer about whom little is known (fig. 323). In 1924 it was purchased by John English, President of the United Baking Company headquartered on Erie Boulevard. The company had an output of 300,000 loaves a year ("Lady Betty" bread was its leading brand), and daily deliveries were made within a radius of seventy miles. The house has the basic outlines of a Colonial Revival hipped-roof house. The elaborate entrance is in keeping with the style (fig. 324). The paired, Ionic columns and the low arch over the door recall a Federal style entrance, but the massiveness of the columns and the elaborate balustrade impart a Georgian feeling. This fusion of styles was the essence of the Colonial Revival. Other elements, however, draw this house away from the Colonial Revival and into a proto-modern style. Broad eaves are reminiscent of Frank Lloyd Wright designs, and flat plaster lends an austerity foreign to the Colonial Revival.

FIG. 321 Sheltered porch of the John Parker house created by thrusting the first floor of the house to the left. There is no historical precedent for such an arrangement.

Possibly, as he was designing the house, the similarity of the broad eaves and plaster to an Italian country house so struck the architect that he chose to include oversized, double brackets under the eaves. Such double brackets on a smaller scale are characteristic of Italian country homes and were ubiquitous in this country in the mid-Victorian period when Italianate architecture was in vogue. The round-arched windows on the first floor also recall the simple arches cut through walls in an abstract ways is part of the Modern movement, but it would also be appropriate to call it a characteristic of the Victorian period.

Thus we see the swinging pendulum of architectural thought. From a medieval lack of concern for anything but comfort from the elements, the Age of Reason developed styles based on rigidly conceived geometric relationships. The Victorian period discarded symmetry and returned to the Romantic picturesque. During the Colonial Revival and Colonial Imitation periods, order again dominated. Residential architecture since that time has seen the pendulum swing again, and the beginnings of that movement are documented in the Realty Plot. Once again, personal considerations, symbolized by the attached garage, dominate in residential architecture. It is intriguing to speculate what the future may hold when the pendulum changes direction yet again.

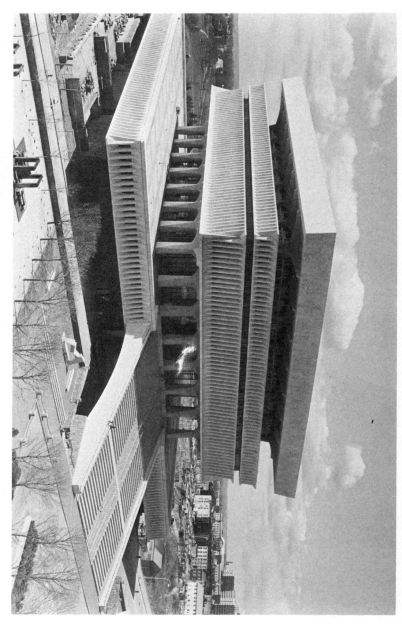

FIG. 322 Cultural Center, Empire State Mall, Albany, New York. Photograph taken while the building was under construction.

FIG. 324 Entrance of the Bower house.

246

FIG. 323 *The Charles DeHart Bower house (1910), 1171 Lowell Road.*

FIG. 325 Postcard view of Douglas Road from
Wendell Avenue. The most distant two houses
have been razed.

Epilogue – In Memoriam

Ernest J. Berggren enjoyed a personal friendship with Henry Ford which grew out of their mutual acquaintance with Thomas Edison. Since he spent a great deal of time in the Menlo Park laboratory in the early days, his recollections played an important part in its restoration in Greenfield Village, Dearborn, Michigan (fig. 326). He wrote on January 20, 1941, two years before his death, "I came to the Menlo Park laboratory as an assistant to Mr. William Carman, the manager of the Office and Accountant, about six months after the first successful test of the incandescent lamp with the carbonized cotton thread. When Edison moved his plant from New York City in 1886 to Schenectady, N.Y., I went with him and became Head Accountant of the plant. In 1910 Edison sent for me to come back to him and become Secretary-Treasurer of his factory in West Orange, N.J., then known as [the] National Phonograph Company. So, here I am, a retired old cripple in my 78th year living on pleasant memories of earlier years. At Menlo Park during the experimental period there was a staff of about fifty men. Today, I understand, there are only three survivors, of which I am one."

William James Foster served for thirty-nine years as a designing engineer and consulting engineer at General Electric (fig. 327). He was selected by the American Institute of Electrical Engineers as the 1931 Lamme Medalist; at the presentation ceremony, Philip L. Alger said, "No one has been more intimately and continuously associated with the development of large electrical machinery during its period of most rapid progress than Mr. W.J. Foster."

Albert L. Rohrer was the Superintendent of General Electric for thirty years (fig. 328). He interviewed an estimated 4000 college graduates who were then hired "on test" with General Electric. His famous "test course" introduced hundreds of

FIG. 326   The Berggren house (c. 1900) shortly before it was demolished.

FIG. 327 The William J. Foster house (c. 1900), early photograph.

FIG. 328 The Albert L. Rohrer house (1900) in the 1950's.

prominent engineers into the electrical industry. Rohrer had wide interests at work and in the community. He organized the apprentice department, the emergency hospital, the works restaurant, and the dental clinic. He was President of the School Board, and he helped establish the Humane Society, the free public library, the Unitarian Society, and the water system. After his retirement at age 75, he went to Guatemala to study Mayan ruins, and he crossed the Syrian desert to stay with archeologists excavating at Ur. A bronze plaque on the front of Building 16 honors his pivotal contributions to General Electric.

Charles P. Steinmetz, "the Modern Jove," "the Thunderer," was the greatest technical expert in American history. He was a genius, a philosopher, and a humanitarian (figs. 329, 330).

Jesse R. Lovejoy was General Manager of Sales and, later, vice-President in charge of sales of General Electric (fig. 331). His outstanding achievement with the company was the creation of a world-wide sales organization.

George E. Emmons was Manager of the Schenectady works for twenty-five years, beginning in 1894 (figs. 332, 333). Besides being responsible for the immense growth of the company during that time, he was also instrumental in the development of the company's plants in other areas.

These men and the houses they lived in are now no more than the mental images that words create. They are part of the heritage of Schenectady which is forever lost. Why were these houses destroyed? In the case of the Steinmetz house, the answer is plainly bureaucratic fumbling. It was slated for restoration as a museum, but while local and state agencies pondered who would control it, the prize was snatched by Vandalism and Neglect. For the others, the reasons are not clear. Some were lost

FIG. 329   *The Charles P. Steinmetz house (1901).*
Photograph taken March 13, 1934.

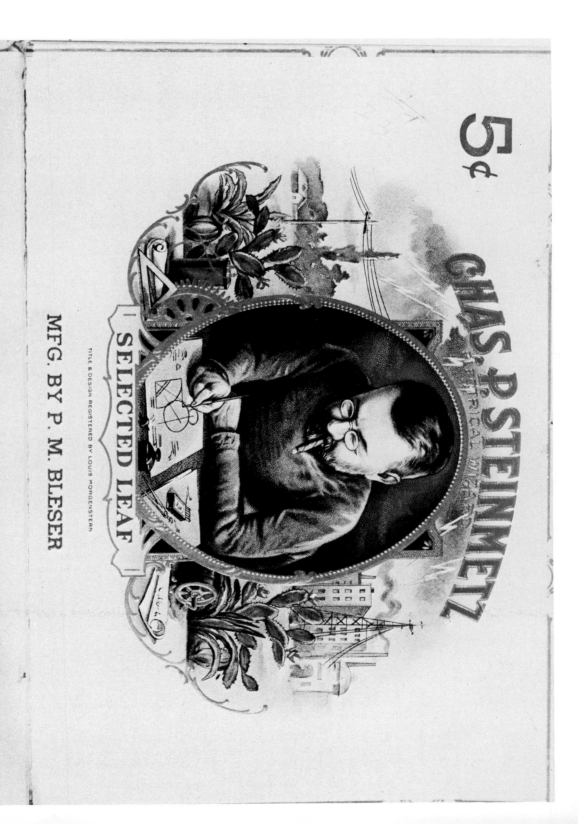

5¢

CHAS. P. STEINMETZ

ELECTRICAL WIZARD

SELECTED LEAF

TITLE & DESIGN REGISTERED BY LOUIS MORGENSTERN

MFG. BY P. M. BLESER

THE LUZON CIGAR CO. INC.

FIG. 330 Cigar box design showing Charles P. Steinmetz. Steinmetz endorsed this brand for a friend who was a local cigar maker. To the end, however, he smoked Blackstone panatelas.

FIG. 332   *The George E. Emmons house (1902).*

FIG. 333   *Gardens of the Emmons house.*

FIG. 331   *The Jesse R. Lovejoy house (c. 1902).*

when past achievements were forgotten and it was thought these large homes were "white elephants." Perhaps because so much of the city's greatness was the result of the ability of its citizens to render old ways obsolete, it judged itself by the same standards and relentlessly discarded any part considered outmoded. More recently, the national mania to obliterate evidence of the past may be part of a primitive instinct to destroy anything which cannot be comprehended. For the future, what concerned Schenectadian could justify inflicting any further injury upon the Enclave of Elegance? The Realty Plot, so painstakingly erected by men who saw a glorious future for the city must be a nidus from which to revitalize Schenectady. No possible good could come from dismantling it.

Bibliography

Much of the factual material used in this book was gathered from old newspapers, documents, and personal communications. Sources for this information included the City History Center, Jay Street, Schenectady, New York, and the Schenectady County Historical Society, Washington Avenue, Schenectady, New York. Biographical information on Dr. Alexanderson and other scientists was supplied by the General Electric Company. The background information on architectural history was learned from Mr. James Kettlewell (see acknowledgements).

In addition to these sources, the following sources were used:

1. *The American Renaissance*, published by the Brooklyn Museum for an exhibit of the same title, Brooklyn, New York, 1979

2. Baxter, W.T., *The House of Hancock; Business in Boston 1724-1775*, Harvard University Press, Cambridge, Mass., 1945

3. Coggeshall, Robert F., *Biography of the Darling Family*, unpublished

4. *The Concise Oxford Dictionary of Quotations*, Oxford Press, 1972

5. Drake, Samuel, *Our Colonial Homes*, Lee and Shepard, Boston, Mass., 1893

6. Economic Study—Capital District Regional Planning Commission

7. Foley, Mary Mix, *The American House*, Harper and Row, New York, 1980

8. Hart, Larry, *Schenectady's Golden Era*, Scotia, New York, 1974

9. Hitchcock, Henry-Russell, *The Architecture of H. H. Richardson and His Times*, Cambridge, Mass., 1936

10. McGehee, Jr., Carden Coleman, *The Planning, Sculpture, and Architecture of Monument Avenue, Richmond, Virginia, 1890-1920*, unpublished thesis, University of Virginia, 1980

11. Miller, John Anderson, *Men and Volts at War*, McGraw-Hill, New York, 1947

12. Miller, John Anderson, *Yankee Scientist: William David Coolidge*, Mohawk Development Service, Scotia, New York, 1963

13. Morrison, Hugh, *Early American Architecture from the First Colonial Settlement to the National Period*, New York, Oxford University Press, 1952

14. *The National Cyclopedia of American Biography*, James T. White Co., New York

15. Pamphlet "Johnson Hall," New York State Parks and Recreation, Albany, New York

16. Poppeliers, J., Chambers, S.A., and Schwartz, N., *What is Style*, Washington, D.C., 1977

17. Prosser, William F., *A History of the Puget Sound Country*, Lewis Pub. Co., 1903

Acknowledgements

Many individuals helped me collect the information to write this book. Past and present residents of the Realty Plot shared their recollections and helped gather information. The staff of the City History Center and the Schenectady County Historical Society devoted considerable time pointing me to the right parts of their collections. Some individuals, however, deserve special mention for their invaluable service "above and beyond" to this project.

James Kettlewell, architectural historian at Skidmore College, spent seven cold hours with me inspecting each house and dictating into a tape recorder.

Angela Catrambone, my secretary, spent many days transcribing these poor quality tapes.

Angela Calabria is responsible for redrawing the original plans, maps, and illustrations in figures 4, 13, 27, 58, 66, 80, 82, 84, 131, 139, 163, 170, 233, 274, 276, 296, 304, and 319 so that they could be reproduced for this book.

Larry Hart, City Historian and author of several books on local history, gave me the encouragement to carry forward with the project.

Frank Gado, English professor at Union College, fearlessly edited the rough draft. As a result, this book is a "real book" and not a high school term paper.

Frank Tedeschi and Edward Bruhn, photographers for over 150 of the illustrations, devoted many more hours than they originally envisioned in performing the difficult task of capturing many well-camouflaged houses on film.

Joseph Hayden, grandson of Charles P. Steinmetz, did the photographic reproduction work of

256

all the old photographs which I unearthed; he dealt patiently with my insistence that every brass button visible in the originals come through to the duplicates.

Louis Navias contributed independent research about the Emmons house, the Waters house, and the Weber family.

Richard Vale also carried on a quiet independent research which netted pictures of the Ely houses and information about Cameron.

Francis Poulin, local history buff, introduced me to a dusty attic in City Hall of which even the City History Center Librarian was unaware. There we spent a profitable day perusing the assessment rolls to determine the construction dates of the early houses.

Neighbors who provided more than their share of information about their ancestors include Harriet Hull, Ruth Bartlett, Thomas Linville, the late Everett Lee, and Harriet Cochrane.

Lastly, Lynne Maston, my wife, spent several days in the County Courthouse searching deeds and proofread the many drafts for content and spelling. Her most important contribution was enduring my daily harangue about this project which lasted for four years.

Photography Credits

Many of the photographs used in this book were donated by individual families to the Realty Plot Association. Other photographs have been used with the gracious permission of the following individuals and organizations.

Albany Institute of History and Art, Albany, NY—21
City of Schenectady History Center, Schenectady, NY—4, 13, 23, 24, 55, 57, 58, 68, 78, 107, 112, 125, 139, 163, 168, 170, 177, 193, 228, 231, 232, 234, 237, 244, 272, 274, 276, 287, 293, 296, 304, 307, 315, 319, 331
Cornell University Libraries, Ithaca, NY—280
Country Life, London, England—16
First Unitarian Society, Schenectady, NY—330
David Gebhard, Santa Barbara, CA—298
The General Electric Company, Schenectady, NY—5, 6, 7, 29, 52, 114, 115, 138, 148, 199, 216, 225, 261, 262, 263, 279, 301, 329
Girl Scouts of the U.S.A., New York, NY—253
Larry Hart, Schenectady, NY—14, 113, 309
House of the Seven Gables, Salem, MA—15
John Hancock Mutual Life Insurance Company, Boston, MA—136
Carden McGehee, Jr., Richmond, VA—159
New York Department of Parks, Recreation, and Historic Preservation, Saratoga-Capital District Region—17
Louis Navias, Schenectady, NY—227
New York Historical Society, New York, NY—2, 8, 18, 63, 260
Office of General Services, New York State, Albany, NY—322
Preservation Society of Newport County, Newport, RI—20
Rockefeller Center, Inc., New York, NY—165
Schenectady County Historical Society, Schenectady, NY—1, 9, 19, 22, 28, 62, 64, 86, 87, 90, 123, 140, 169, 184, 185, 212, 218, 229, 283, 325
Schenectady County Public Library, Schenectady, NY—326
Schenectady Trust Company, Schenectady, NY—3
Robert C. Twombly, New York, NY—284
Union College, Schenectady, NY—288, 328
Photograph Collection, University of Washington Library, Pierson and Company Photographers—195
White Studio, Schenectady, NY—53, 54, 224

Index

Architects and Their Houses

Aftel, S.
  Jonathan Levi
Atkinson, E. G.
  Edgar Dickinson
  Charles Fair
Blanchard, A. E.
  Oscar Junggren
Clarke and Howe
  William Ely (1360 Lenox Rd)
Clif, Chris
  Horatio Glen
Comstock, F. L.
  Abraham Brubacher
Crabtree, Walter P.
  Henry Boardman
  Edward Peck
Derby, Robinson and Shepard
  Edwin Baldwin
Edward, Reed, and Greco Co.
  A. G. Darling
Ellet, Thomas Harlan
  D. C. Prince
Finch, Oren
  Andrew Averrett
  Thomas Brown
  Arthur Mann
  George C. Moon
  Howard Sargent
  Garrett Veeder
  John Weber
Frost, Briggs, and Chamberlain
  Edward Priest
Fuller and Robinson
  Ernst Berg
Jones Newhall
  Herbert Wirt
Lindley, A. G. Co.
  Charles Bower
  James Hooker
  Frank Hoppman
  McDermott children
  James Parker
  John Parker
  John Riley
  Stephen Visscher
Maloney, J. E.
  Arthur Bradt

Mynderse, William T. B.
  Anna Benham
  Arthur Buck
  William Ely (1141 Adams Rd.)
  Emmet-McNaughton
  Haigh-Salmon
  Frances Haskins
  John Horman
  Knight-Rice
  Roy C. Muir
  Samuel Stewart
  Charles G. Van Brunt
Nichols, L. Rodman
  Henry Horstmeyer
  Albert Vedder
Reynolds, M. L.
  Henry Reist
Rossiter, E. K.
  George E. Emmons
  Martin P. Rice
Russell and Rice
  John Bellamy Taylor (1279 Lowell Rd.)
  Henry P. Walker, Jr.
Stephans, W. E.
  J. C. Hardie
Taylor, G.
  Abraham Gifford
Van Rensselaer, Cortland
  John Bartlett
  Warren Conover
  H. A. Hanson
  Oliver Kline
  Percival Lewin
Wallach, Ekin
  George Whittlesey (1112 Lowell Rd.)